MISTER PRESIDENT:
The Story of Ronald Reagan

revised edition

Mary Virginia Fox

ENSLOW PUBLISHERS, INC.

Bloy St. & Ramsey Ave.　　P.O. Box 38
Box 777　　　　　　　　　Aldershot
Hillside, N.J.　07205　　Hants GU12 6BP
U.S.A.　　　　　　　　　　　　U.K.

Cover Photo: Mike Evans, The White House

Copyright © 1986, 1982 by Mary Virginia Fox

Library of Congress Cataloging in Publication Data

Fox, Mary Virginia.
Mister President: the story of Ronald Reagan. -- Rev. ed.

Includes index.
Summary: A biography of the former motion picture actor elected fortieth President of the United States in 1980 and again in 1984.
1. Reagan, Ronald— Juvenile literature. 2. Presidents—United States—Biography—Juvenile literature. [1. Reagan, Ronald. 2. Presidents]
I. Title.

E877.F69 1986   973.927'092'4 [B] [92]   86-4420
ISBN 0-89490-130-3

Printed in the United States of America

10 9 8 7 6 5 4 3

"For such a little bit of a fat Dutchman, he makes a whale of a lot of noise."

That's what Ronald Reagan's father said on that day February 6, 1911 when his son was born. The nickname "Dutch" was to last, although the baby's mother thought Ronald Wilson Reagan much better, "Ronnie" for short.

Two-year-old brother Neil wouldn't even look at the baby. He'd been promised a sister, and he was disappointed.

Reagan was born in a small apartment above the H. C. Pitney General Store. That's where his father, Jack Reagan, sold shoes. The town was Tampico, Illinois. There was only one block of paved street in the whole community of 1200 people. But it was a friendly town.

The Reagan family had very little money, although the boys never remember considering themselves poor. There weren't any people in town who could call themselves wealthy, so it was hard to imagine what it would be like to have everything you wanted. Besides, their mother was always finding someone who needed help.

"When there is someone who has more troubles than you have, it puts you on the top of the heap," Reagan later explained.

It wasn't long before they moved to larger quarters across the railroad tracks. Their new home had a front porch with a clattery swing that was fun to pump. Nearby was a park with an old Civil War cannon that could be used for imaginary battles.

But the next few years brought more moves. Neil had long ago given up his disappointment over having a brother. The two boys were nearly always together. Brothers can fill the gap of loneliness when moves separate them from friends.

It was a closely-knit family, although one combining opposite temperaments. The boys always called their father "Jack." He had dark hair and was as muscular as an athlete. He believed strongly in the rights of the working man and was proud of being a Democrat. Although not a strict churchgoer, he bragged of his Irish Catholic background.

Jack believed that all men were created equal and that a man's own ambition determined what happened to him. He had no tolerance for those who held prejudice. Reagan remembers that he and his brother were probably the only kids in town not permitted to see the film classic "Birth of a Nation."

"It deals with the Ku Klux Klan against colored folks," Jack explained. "I won't have anyone in this family see it."

Another time his father walked out of a hotel because they wouldn't allow Jews. It meant he had to sleep in a car overnight.

Jack Reagan was restless, always hoping for a better job, but he had one serious problem, which he was always battling. He loved to drink. There were times when he wasn't able to control this sickness. Nelle Reagan tried to explain to her children that their father needed love and help. They were not to condemn him for this weakness. In every other way he lived up to being a caring and conscientious husband and father.

During those times when he couldn't work, Nelle Reagan turned to her faith to help her through times of stress. "The Lord will provide." She was a staunch member of the Protestant Christian Church.

Nelle Reagan was small, with auburn hair and blue eyes. She was mild-mannered, yet had a strict code she expected the family to follow. She impressed on them the value of hard work and piety. Nelle was sure everyone loved her just because she loved them. There was never a thought that people might be talking behind her back. It wasn't easy to hide the fact that Jack Reagan had his drunken moments, but if she ever felt bitterness, she hid it.

Neither parent had attended high school, but Nelle tried to make up for it with her love of books. She had a flair as a performer. She gave regular dramatic readings for various ladies' societies, and she occasionally directed plays if she could recruit a few neighbors to perform in the local "opera house", which was a fine name for a rather drafty second-floor meeting hall used for all kinds of public gatherings.

The boys often were there for rehearsals and for the big pot of oyster stew that made the evening the social, not professional, event it was.

There were other lighter moments, as when Jack Reagan was the star of the Parent Teachers Association skit dressed in a crepe paper hula skirt and wig. Nobody could forget Jack. Nelle was the serious one, but she could go along with these crazy stunts and seem to enjoy them.

Nelle was a public-spirited woman who visited prisoners in the county jail and who rounded up donations for Christmas baskets for the poor—frequently when the Reagan Christmas wasn't much better than the Christmas for those she was helping.

Nelle was the doer, Jack the dreamer. But he never could seem to match life with what he wanted. When he heard there was a job opening in Chicago with Marshall Fields Department Store, he packed up the family overnight and headed for this wonderful new opportunity.

He was a good salesman, and he had scientifically studied the proper fitting of shoes. He always carried a drawing of the bones of the foot to explain to his customers just what type of shoes they should be wearing. He planned on owning his own store someday. In the meantime there was the excitement of living in a big city.

It turned out to be one of the most miserable periods of their lives. Jack's salary was small, the cost of living comparatively high. Neil remembers being sent to the grocery store with his little brother to ask for liver for the

Ronald Reagan (third from left) is shown with his parents and his older brother Neil.

cat. The liver was for Sunday dinner. The Reagans had no cat. A soup pot lasted the rest of the week.

On Saturdays, when there was a football game at the nearby University of Chicago stadium, Nelle Reagan would send the boys out to sell popcorn she'd popped and bagged in their own kitchen. Even with a salesman's discount, they were unable to buy clothes from the fancy department store. She made their own.

They were forced to live in a small apartment where they had to put quarters in a gas meter every few hours to provide heat and light. The sputtering gas jet caused more than one problem.

There was a day when Jack was at work and Nelle was out on one of her goodwill trips. She was gone longer than expected. Both Neil and Ron were scared. They decided to go out in search of their parents, but first they very carefully blew out the gas lamp. When their mother returned she was frantic. The room was filled with gas. Her children were missing. When the boys finally did return, she lost her temper and they lost their desire to sit on the seat of their pants for a day.

No one in the family was happy with Chicago. They dreamed of returning to a small town, to the very life they'd tried to escape. When Jack Reagan finally found a job in Galesburg, they moved again.

In Galesburg they were back to a landscape of green trees and red-brick streets. It was easier to learn nature lessons here than in the cement-covered world of the big city.

Those lessons had a boost from the treasures found in the attic of their rented bungalow. The previous owner had left a large collection of birds' eggs and butterflies. They were carefully stored in a glass case. The boys decided to add to the museum with their own collection of an emerald-green grass snake, spiders, crickets, and whatever could be found in the vacant lot across the street.

Jack Reagan decided he'd prefer they have more usual pets. He gave them each a set of prize pigeons. They also raised rabbits. The collection multiplied quickly.

Neil and Ron made a brief attempt at putting on a circus with their wildlife. They enlisted the help of one of their friends who had a goat. The production lasted only for two performances because of lack of an audience. When it came time a few weeks later to eat some of the performers, Ron would have nothing to do with it.

"He couldn't go for the killing," said Neil.

From Galesburg they moved to Monmouth, a pretty college town with rolling hills, but soon it was back to Tampico. Nelle Reagan always found a way to set up housekeeping and make the family feel at home.

One of the homiest places young Ron found was provided by the elderly couple who lived next door. They had no children of their own. Ronnie and Neil were their substitute family. The ten-cent-a-week allowance Aunt Emma and Uncle Jim (as they were called) gave the boys was considered sheer luxury.

The couple owned and operated the Tampico jewelry store, with its curious stock of new and antique treasures.

There was a pleasant musty smell to the place and a soothing sound from the dozens of ticking clocks. Ronnie was given permission to make his own private hideaway in a corner of the shop. As an added treat, Aunt Emma furnished an almost unlimited supply of hot chocolate.

Another special memory Reagan cherishes is the time he and his brother spent on the farm owned by the Lutyens, friends of their parents. There were animals to play with. The boys hauled water to the men in the fields thrashing grain and were rewarded with heaping helpings of fried chicken, pie, and watermelon.

"Those were the happiest days of my life," Reagan later admitted.

Even before Ronald Reagan started school at the age of five, he had learned to put letters together. Nelle took time every night to read to her children. Ron followed every word with a finger and finally realized he could put all the funny black marks together as words. His mother was so proud she brought in neighbors to listen to her prodigy.

Later in school, the prodigy did not make spectacular marks. No one had discovered what his problem was until one afternoon when they were all out riding in the country. Neil could read the highway signs. Ron couldn't. His mother suggested he try on her glasses. Suddenly the letters jumped into focus. Faces weren't blurred. Trees had leaves. There was texture and color to everything.

He immediately was taken to be fitted with his own black-rimmed spectacles. School was now a breeze, although he still had a problem in sports. Standing at the plate waiting for a pitch to come was a frightening experience. The ball would appear out of nowhere about two feet in front of him. Football was his love, but Ron still was small for his age. Neil proved to be the star on the field.

By this time the two year's difference in age was pushing them apart. Ron knew he had to find friends of his own. It wasn't all that hard. Ron was never one to be a loner. The closest friend he had at this time was Monkey Winchell. Monkey's father owned a store on the main street in town. The family lived above it.

One day the boys discovered Mr. Winchell's pump shotgun in the closet. For no reason, except curiosity, Monkey put the butt of the gun on the floor and pulled the trigger. Nothing happened, but then there was the temptation of one more try. Ron pumped it once and gave it back to his friend. The next action blasted a hole in the ceiling. Plaster showered down upon them. The parents burst in on the scene of two frightened youngsters trying to look unconcerned as they read their Sunday school quarterly.

Reagan remembers that the punishment wasn't as bad as the unpleasantness of the potato incident. Jack had bought a whole carload of half-spoiled produce at a bargain price. It was up to the boys to sort the good from the bad. The smell of the squishy rotten potatoes made them gag, but they were kept at it for a week. It is no wonder that potatoes are not the favorite food of the President of the United States.

When Reagan was nine the family moved once again. Jack had found a partner to finance a fine shoe store in Dixon, Illinois. He was to be the manager. For once, their lives seemed to be fitting together smoothly. With an easing of worries, Jack's drinking bouts were almost eliminated.

They were able to settle into a routine. Ronald Reagan was to live in Dixon until he was twenty-one years old. He affectionately claims it as his home town. It was this upbringing in a small Midwestern town that was to shape his views for all the years that followed.

Ronald Reagan at two years of age.
Wisconsin Center for Film and Theater Research

About 10,000 people lived in the pleasant rural community ninety miles west of Chicago. Arching over the main street, Galena Avenue, was a wooden sign erected as a memorial to those who had died in World War I. Tall elm trees shaded the parkways. The Rock River flowed through the middle of town.

A 320-acre park had been donated to the city by the family of James Russell Lowell. In the summer it was a favorite spot for swimming. In the winter, when the freeze came before snow, the skating area was endless. The trick was to skate hard against the wind, then spread your coat to sail back. There also was assassination hockey, a game of tag that made Reagan an excellent skater. He was great at open-ice dodging.

The elementary school and high school overlooked the river. The buildings had been built during the time of the Civil War, of brick, with high ceilings and creaking wooden floors. Here there was a sense of belonging. Everyone was known by a first or nickname. There were no strangers.

Ron was now called "Dutch," and Neil had somehow picked up the tag "Moon."

There were Saturday Western thrillers at the Family Theater, and of course there was football. The Reagans lived on the south side of the river on Hennepin Avenue. Across the street lived the O'Malleys, with Eddie and George matching the ages of Dutch and Moon. With four players—one center, one ball carrier, and two on the defensive line—they manufactured as much excitement as two full squads in battle.

When Dutch started high school in 1927, he was five feet three inches tall, weighing one hundred and eight pounds. He was skinny, nearsighted, all elbows and Adam's apple. He still wore thick black-rimmed glasses. His hair hung over his forehead when he wasn't pushing it back with his fingers. Yet his face was marked by handsome features.

He was conscientious and serious. Ronald Reagan is remembered as being almost too perfect a boy to be true. He was friendly and courteous. There were few times he ever needed punishment, there being no more pranks like shooting holes in ceilings. He took care of chores around the house and, for pay, did jobs around the neighborhood. At fourteen he was paid thirty-five cents an hour for digging foundations, for a construction company.

His brother Moon remembers that Dutch didn't crack a book all that often, yet he had such a fantastic memory he did very well in school. That memory has been a blessing to him since, when having to memorize a movie script or a political speech.

Then it gave him more time for the fun things he wanted to do. Football was the greatest challenge. That's where heroes were made, and it was the one sport "where a man can physically throw himself, his full body, into combat with another man," Reagan later explained. It wasn't that he was anxious for a fight but for a way to prove himself.

It took a lot of proving. Dutch was too near-sighted to catch a ball and too small still to play in the line. That didn't keep him from running plays and drills every moment he could with the bench substitutes. He would charge down the field with enthusiasm and jump into the battle without fear. There were bruises and a black eye or two, but no dimming of enthusiasm. He'd make the team yet, and he did. His junior year he earned the right to wear a uniform.

Jack Reagan was proud of his youngest son's competitive spirit, but there was never a relationship of father and son doing things together. In many ways the family split two-by-two. When Jack felt the need to attend mass, it was Moon he took to the Catholic Church. Dutch always went with his mother to the Christian Church, also called the Disciples of Christ church.

It was here he met Margaret Cleaver, the first love of his life. She was a sparkling brunette, daughter of the minister. Reagan was not without a rival. His friend Dick McNicol, quarterback and captain of the football team, fell for the same girl.

Margaret handled the situation astutely. The fellows took turns with dates, but as the months went by, it was obvious that she had a favorite and it was Dutch.

When it came time for the senior banquet, Dick, nobly, recognized what was happening and said to Dutch, "I think Margaret has made her choice."

Dutch was relieved that there were no hard feelings. It's rare that friendship could stand such a test, but all three remained friends.

Although football was his main interest, Reagan was busy with a lot of other activities. He was too poor to buy a Boy Scout uniform, but there were overnight hikes with the YMCA group and swimming lessons at the Y pool.

He easily passed his lifesaving test and was hired seven years in a row as lifeguard at Lowell Park. The hours were long, from early morning until dark. Dutch admits that he found a way once or twice to get the swimmers out of the water a little early. He succeeded by tossing a pebble into the water and suggesting the splash was made by a river rat.

His lunch, which he didn't have to pay for, was brought to him. With no time to spend his money, he was able to put it aside for college.

Ronald Reagan had a record of saving seventy-seven lives during the months he was on duty. He remembers that many of those he pulled from the water were angry that he'd come to their rescue. Some felt he was just trying to play the part of hero. However, there was a treacherous current when the sluices were opened in the dam downstream. Most swimmers were unaware of the sudden change of conditions.

In high school Reagan wrote for the school yearbook,

and he took an active part in student government. He showed his leadership role even then by being elected president of his senior class.

He also showed a flair for dramatics. His English teacher, P. J. Fraser, who also was the drama coach, has some interesting recollections of his famous student.

"He was an above-average student, quite interested in English and literature. He was original and creative. And he

DONALD REAGAN
"Dutch"
"Life is just one grand sweet song,
so start the music."
Pres. N. S. Student Body 4; Pres.
2; Play 3, 4; Dram. Club 3, 4, Pres.
4; Fresh.-Soph. Drama Club 1, 2,
Pres. 2; Football 3, 4; Annual Staff;
Hi-Y 3, 4, Vice-Pres. 4; Art 1, 2;
Lit. Contest 2; Track 2, 3.

Ronald "Dutch" Reagan's entry in the Dixon High School Yearbook for 1928 contains a proofreading error.

Dixon High School, Dixon, Illinois

had a quality that not too many high school kids have: he finished what he started."

It was also noted that he had an interest in people, a fine quality for a politician as well as an actor.

Reagan himself has some interesting comments about Fraser's "knack of quietly leading us into a performance, of making us think our roles, instead of acting them mechanically."

His junior year Reagan played Ricky, the young son in Philip Barry's play "You and I." His father was played by his friendly rival Dick McNicol. The next year Reagan was the villain in George Bernard Shaw's "Captain Applejack."

"The fact was, I suppose, that I just liked showing off," Reagan said of his early acting career.

Moon Reagan had passed up college to work in a cement plant. Dutch didn't know what he wanted to do with his life, but the cement plant was not to be part of it. He was one of the few students in the rural town of Dixon in the late 1920's who planned to go on to college. He had listened often to his mother's speeches. "Education can't guarantee success, but it can give you an extra chance."

Reagan had never complained of his family's poverty, but he was determined to climb the ladder of financial security.

Secretly he had thought of becoming an actor, but few people in the Midwest at that time considered it a practical career. Even P. J. Fraser advised against it. Reagan put that dream out of his mind.

With $400 in his savings account and a brand new, shiny black steamer trunk, he headed for Eureka College a few miles away.

He had chosen Eureka College for three reasons. He could afford the tuition, it was close to home, and, most important, that was where Margaret Cleaver was going.

It was a pretty campus with five main buildings built in a semicircle. They were of red brick with white-framed windows. There was even an ivy-covered Gothic tower. Two hundred and fifty students made up the entire enrollment.

Dutch Reagan was now six feet tall, weighing in at his all-time high of 175 pounds. With his enthusiasm for sports, he earned an athletic scholarship that paid for half of his $180-tuition and guaranteed him a job. He raked lawns, washed dishes, and waited on tables to meet his other college expenses. To this day President Reagan feels that young people should earn their right to education rather than have the government pay for it.

As in high school, Reagan was always into activities. He joined Tau Kappa Epsilon fraternity, thanks to a boy-friend of Margaret's sister. He immediately became one of the leaders of his class. However, he still was not picked to be on the first-string football team, which bothered him considerably.

Every Saturday there were battles in the "Little 19," a conference of small colleges in the prairies of the Midwest. The football field was flanked with wooden bleachers filled on weekends with the entire student body and a few of the townspeople.

Howard Short, manager of Eureka's team, remembers Dutch Reagan as "the freshman who stuck with the football squad all fall although he never even got a first-class jersey."

But Dutch showed up as a star in other fields. He joined the freshman debating team and was recognized very early in the year as a good speaker who could handle himself well even without a memorized prepared speech. Because of his talents here, he was selected as freshman representative on the student council. In this role he participated in his first "political battle."

Eureka was a coed college supported by the Disciples of Christ church. No bars were allowed in the town of Eureka, and no liquor was sold within the town's city limits.

Anyone caught smoking or drinking was expelled. Ballroom dancing was considered evil. College President Wilson had penalized students caught attending the weekly family-night dances at the American Legion hall, even when with their parents. He took away grade points for graduation.

There was a strong feeling among the students and faculty that rules should be relaxed and President Wilson dismissed. However there seemed no way to attack the church-oriented school because everyone had known the rules before they enrolled.

The year Reagan arrived on campus, President Wilson announced that to balance the budget a number of courses would have to be eliminated. This was just the cause the students had been waiting for to bind themselves together in actions against the administration. A petition was drawn up requesting the dismissal of President Wilson. Many of the faculty, whose jobs were being cut, were in sympathy with the students' position.

The petition was duly presented to the trustees of the college. Everyone waited anxiously for the verdict. The trustees sided with President Wilson against the students. They hoped that peace could be achieved simply by dismissing the problem from their own minds. This was not to be.

Word reached the student leaders late at night that their petition had been rejected. They took matters into their own hands. Someone rang the campus bell calling everyone to a meeting in the chapel. Students poured out of the dorms, some with coats over their nightclothes.

The building had been built to accommodate the 250 students enrolled. Many more than that crowded into the room that night: Eureka graduates from around the town also gathered. Many of them were unhappy with Wilson, not only because of the strict rules of the college, but because the college president had suggested in one of his more recent speeches that the town of Eureka was too small to support such a college. They were afraid that his cutting of the curriculum would indeed be the end of the school. Everyone there had come to demand the president's resignation.

Speeches were made by several student leaders criticizing the administration. Then it was time for Reagan, the freshman representative, to speak. He had been asked to introduce a strike vote. It was felt that a senior might be accused of having a special interest in avoiding cutbacks that could keep upperclassmen from graduating if the courses were eliminated. The plea should come from a freshman who was just starting to build a four-year program of study.

Seventeen-year-old Reagan stepped to the podium and gave an impassioned plea for all to stand behind their beliefs. Under new guidance the college could survive, even lead, as an institution of higher learning. He called upon everyone to show their loyalty with action. Their demands had been ignored. Let everyone know the strength of their convictions on the issues by boycotting classes.

Reagan recalls, "I discovered that night that an audience has a feel to it, and in the parlance of theater, that audience and I were together."

He was not the one who led the revolt. He was "Paul Revere sounding the alarm," as he put it.

His motion was adopted unanimously. When classes resumed most of the students stayed away. Professors joined the protest, taking the roll and reporting that none of the missing students were absent. It was a complete defiance of rules. And in a college where rules were never broken without expulsion, it was a daring and dangerous action.

President Wilson finally got the message. Life could never be the same on the sleepy little campus. On December seventh he resigned.

The students met again and graciously thanked the president for his actions. They then sent a letter to the trustees stating that they "did not presume to dictate further what the actions of the trustees shall be in any matters affecting the policy and program of the school. . . We love Eureka College."

That ended the student unrest, but it had been such a daring break with the conservative traditions of the school that it was the talk of the campus for months. Reagan was reminded of these actions later in his life when, as Governor of California, he had to deal with striking students.

The rest of Reagan's college life settled into a much more normal routine—normal for the times when college was a four-year blissful period of growing up, where books and socializing had little to do with what was happening off campus. The pleasant life of Eureka had screened out the political unrest of the big cities. There were no radicals on soapboxes calling for the overthrow of the government.

The Depression had hit everyone more or less equally in this part of the country. Simple campus social life became even more so. Few had cars. A fellow didn't need to feel cheap about asking his date to join him at the local drugstore for a five-cent cherry phosphate. Dutch and Margaret saw a lot of each other, but their plans for the

Teenager Ronald Reagan
worked as a lifeguard.

*Wisconsin Center for Film
and Theater Research*

future did not include marriage. They were dating others.

At the fraternity house the fellows played pinochle. The stakes were usually a penalty for the loser. Most often the loser was required to walk the ten blocks downtown to bring back the hamburgers and malted milks they'd all ordered.

Dutch proved he was willing to tackle almost anything. He and two friends, Bud Cole and Elmer Fisher, decided one day that the fraternity needed a new dining area. They ripped out everything in the basement to prepare for remodeling.

As Cole later remembers, "We mainly tore things down and someone with skill put things back, but without Dutch the job would never have gotten started."

The Depression years claimed another victim. Jack Reagan's Fashion Boot Shop finally went out of business, which left Dutch completely on his own for funds. In addition to washing dishes at the fraternity, he worked in the kitchen of the girls' dormitory. Every Saturday he scrubbed cupboards, the floors, whatever jobs the housemother had listed on the bulletin board. When he was through, she would check and recheck his work.

Life wasn't easy, but he was having a great time. He kept telling his brother about all the activities, making life sound perhaps a bit more exciting than it was.

When he came home at the end of his junior year, he told Moon that he had made arrangements for Moon to enter Eureka, having lined up an athletic scholarship and a part-time job for him. Moon was less than enthusiastic. He felt he should keep his job as long as he had one.

When the next semester was starting, Moon came home from the cement plant one night and found his brother's steamer trunk in the middle of the bedroom.

"I thought Dutch had left for school," he said to his mother.

"He has, but your brother left this in case you changed your mind. He packed up his own things in cardboard boxes."

That trunk had been one of Dutch's prized possessions. Moon spent the rest of the night considering his future. He had been working with an elderly immigrant whose health had been ruined by working in the grimy limestone dust. The years ahead were leading nowhere.

The next day Moon Reagan packed and headed for Eureka. He joined his brother's fraternity and soon became one of a close circle of friends Dutch had already gathered around him. There were Pebe Leitch, Bud Cole, and a dozen others.

Each year there was a homecoming show when the fraternities and sororities each put on a skit. Reagan is remembered for one hilariously funny imitation of a radio sportscaster.

Whenever there was a play, he was always on cast call. It was at this time that Reagan became seriously interested in acting. The drama teacher was Miss Ellen Marie Johnston. His high school teacher P. J. Fraser had nurtured his earliest talents. Miss Johnston had only to give Reagan a chance on the stage and he made the most of it. She was an excellent coach. Her record proves it.

During Reagan's junior year she entered her group in the

annual one-act play contest at Northwestern University. Hundreds of colleges and universities from all over the country were competing. Much to everyone's surprise, the Eureka players were one of an even dozen groups to be invited to Evanston, Illinois to give their performance.

Miss Johnson had selected Edna St. Vincent Millay's fantasy *Aria de Capo,* which dealt with the foolishness of war. Grecian costumes were copied from ancient sculpture and sewed together by coed volunteers.

Reagan played one of the Greek shepherd-boys. His high spot was a death scene where he was strangled by his friend Bud Cole. "No actor can ask for more," Reagan has

Eureka College building.

Eureka College, Eureka Illinois

said. "Dying is the way to live in the theater."

When it came time for the awards, the Eureka players placed second. When individual awards, five in all, were handed out, the name "Ronald Reagan" was announced. He sat for a moment in stunned silence. Then he fairly leaped to the stage. Reagan remembers that this recognition was one of the most exciting and unexpected events of his life. He returned to campus with a taste of glory.

The only dream left unfulfilled was on the football field. Dutch had played his heart out in practice his freshman year without notable success. "I told everyone who would listen that the coach didn't like me," Reagan remembers. "I needed a damn good kick in the keister, but how can you kick something that's permanently planted on a bench?"

It was teammate Bud Cole who helped him with some fine playing tips during scrimmage. Cole had earned his letter at Northwestern University and then dropped out of college to play pro ball for a year before entering Eureka. He had the experience to decipher plays. He did a great job of predicting the action.

Watching the signal caller and the stance of the backs on the opposing varsity, he'd whisper to his right guard, who was Dutch at the time, "Go straight across. They'll try a reverse to suck you in."

Following advice and hitting hard, Dutch's playing came to the attention of coach Ralph McKenzie. Reagan was elevated to first string guard next to Pebe Leitch, the right tackle, who was team captain, and his roommate in the fraternity house.

"Dutch was not an outstanding football player, but he was a good plugger, dedicated, put out a lot, and had a lot of spirit and desire," Coach McKenzie remembers.

There were other activities too. Dutch was a reporter on the student newspaper, and he served as feature editor of the yearbook. He was the head cheerleader during the basketball season and was elected president of the Student Senate and the Booster Club.

In later years Reagan spoke with enthusiasm about his college. "One thing about Eureka, you can't remain anonymous. Students in the big assembly-line diploma mills can spend four years admittedly getting a good education, but never stretching themselves to discover if they could participate in a play, sing in a glee club, make a team, or serve in a campus elective office. In a small college everyone is needed and there is no place to hide. If you make it in Eureka, it's because your fellow students know you, not because they don't. And if you can make it under those circumstances you can make it anywhere."

His teachers made a big difference too. "They honestly wanted you to succeed and taught you how to think, not what to think."

With all of Dutch's extra activities there wasn't much time left for studying, he admits, but his grades never got below the C average required for participation in sports. He was majoring in economics and sociology, taking a general course that would prepare him for what-he-did-not-know.

The time for graduation came, not with a feeling of relief that a milestone had been passed, but with reluctance to leave the ivy-clad walls and close friends. A way of life was ending. The next step was frightening. Reagan was broke, in debt, and without a glimmer of a job.

The summer of 1932 he went back to his job as life guard at Lowell Park. It was the only way he knew of to earn and save two hundred dollars in a few weeks. Most of his classmates were out of work. There was plenty of time to ponder the future. He made a list of possible careers, but he always came back to one: he wanted to be in some kind of show business.

Broadway and Hollywood were a long way away. Where else could he turn? There was only one answer, radio. In those days Chicago was the big-time center of the broadcasting industry. Reagan decided to give it a try. He hitchhiked the ninety miles to the city. Thanks to a friend who was studying medicine in Chicago, he had a bed. The next morning he started out knocking on doors. His first stop was NBC. The receptionist informed him interviews were only given on Thursdays. At CBS he told them that he already had an appointment with the rival network but thought he'd drop by to see what other offers were available. He didn't impress a soul.

While at CBS, he had a chance to watch some of the announcers at work through the windows of the visitors' gallery. He was awed by the professionalism he was seeing. His confidence hit a new low.

However he was back at NBC on Thursday. The interview was brief, but the advice was excellent. "Get some experience in the sticks before you try to tackle big time radio in Chicago."

He returned home sadder but wiser. He hated to admit to his family that his aspirations had been crushed. It was brother Moon who put him back in a hopeful mood. He suggested that Dutch take out a map and make a one day tour of the towns within a seventy-five mile radius. The family Oldsmobile would hold up for that much touring.

Davenport, Iowa was just within that circle. Here was a small station with the call letters WOC, which stood for World of Chiropractic. It shared program time with larger station WHO headquartered in Des Moines. The studio was located on the top floor of the building which housed the Palmer School of Chiropractics. For a month they had been advertising for an announcer.

The man Reagan saw was the program director, a Scotsman named Peter MacArthur. He was badly crippled with arthritis, having to walk with a cane. MacArthur was known for his temper and strong language. Reagan felt like using a few sizzling words of his own when he found he had just missed out on the job. The position had been filled the day before from a pool of ninety-four applicants. If he had just come here instead of to Chicago . . .

Without thanking the man for his time, Dutch stamped

out of the office muttering out loud, "How does a guy ever get to be a sports announcer if he can't even get inside a station?"

The door to the elevator opened and Reagan was about to enter when he heard MacArthur's thumping cane and his blustery voice shouting, "Not so fast there. Didn't ye hear me callin' ye? Now what was it ye said about sports?"

It was the first time in all of Reagan's job hunting that he had ever mentioned his lofty ambition to be a sports announcer.

"Do ye perhaps know football?" MacArthur asked.

Reagan breathed a little easier. "I played for eight years, sir."

"Hmm, do ye think you could tell me about a game and make me really see it?"

Reagan grinned. "Sure." This wasn't going to be a fraternity skit. Could he really do it?

Dutch followed the program director into a studio heavily draped with blue velvet, the customary way to soundproof a room in those days. He was instructed to watch for the red light. When it went on he was to start talking.

"Tell us about a game and make me see it."

With that MacArthur left the room. Dutch was alone in front of the mike. He picked out the fourth quarter of a game he had played his senior year at Eureka. He knew the plays and the players. What he had to do was translate the picture in his mind into words, words that would bring alive the excitement of the real action.

He spoke for twenty minutes. When he was through he

was wringing wet and hanging on to the microphone for support. MacArthur entered the studio grinning. "Ye did it."

He explained to Reagan that the station had a sponsor to broadcast four University of Iowa games. "Ye be here a week from Saturday, and I'll give ye five dollars and bus fare. If ye do all right on that one, ye'll do the others."

Just to make sure the young recruit wouldn't spoil the day, a staff announcer went along too. He was to take care of the pre-game patter. It was the first time Reagan had ever been in a press box. As the stands began to fill, his nervousness mounted. His friends from Dixon would be listening.

The staff anouncer read some statistics from cue cards, but soon he was saying, "And now to bring you the play-by-play action, here is Ronald Reagan."

"How do you do ladies and gentlemen. We are speaking to you from high atop the Memorial Stadium at the University of Iowa, looking down from the west stands. It's a gusty day with the winds out of the north."

This type of opening became part of his style, letting the audience see the setting as well as the play.

During the first quarter he played it straight, sticking to facts, making no personal comments on the play of the game. Then as prearranged, he turned the mike back to the regular announcer. The staff man was good at ad-libbing, but his knowledge of the game was limited. When he began to run out of words he hauled out press clippings to read. Reagan offered by sign to lend a hand. The announcer was relieved. Dutch took it upon himself to analyze some of the key plays and suggest what to look for in the last half. This kind of knowledgeable, personal reporting was just what the director had been looking for.

When he was through, Dutch had word from MacArthur that his work was not only satisfactory, it was good. He would be continuing to broadcast the remaining three games. In fact, he was to receive double the salary, ten dollars a game, plus transportation. That wasn't exactly going to pay for food and lodging, but he was now a pro.

He continued to look for work. It was the first of the year that a call came from station WHO. Two staff announcers at the Des Moines, Iowa studio were leaving. Did he want the job? The salary was one hundred dollars a month.

He jumped at the chance. This was NBC's clear-channel station that could be heard in Iowa, Missouri, Minnesota, and northern Illinois. And that salary wasn't anything to jeer about, not when a meal ticket good for three meals a day, six days a week cost $3.65, and a new made-to-measure suit with two pairs of pants came to $18.50.

He read news releases and weather reports, and occasionally he was given an assignment to interview a celebrity, but his chief talent was as sports announcer. Besides football, he announced track meets and baseball games. In the days of budget cutting and not-easily-portable electronic equipment, it was cheaper to broadcast from the station rather than the stands.

His desk was centered in a tiny six-by-eight foot studio next to a room with a teletype machine. There was a big window between the two rooms. When a burst of news came in over the wire, it was handed to him through a slot in the window. On the paper might be written a very brief description of the play of a baseball game. It was up to Reagan to fill in the details as if he were there.

The message might read, "Hartnett singles to right."

Reagan would describe the pitcher as looking to his left toward the runner at first base. "He tugs at his cap, he hesitates. Now he brings his arms up. Here comes the windup. It's a pitch, low to the inside. Hartnett swings. It's a solid hit. Hartnett sprints down the baseline and slides to safety."

Reagan's voice would mount to a climax of excitement. The engineer assistant at the studio would have read the Western Union message as he handed it to Reagan. He was standing poised, ready to crack two pieces of wood together to imitate the sound of the bat on ball as Reagan called the play. Then he'd turn up a phonograph record of the crowd noise cheering. It was so real few people realized the announcer wasn't right in the stands watching the play of the game.

Reagan was one of the best play-by-play men in the business. He never was at a loss for words, even once when a mechanical failure in the middle of the game cut off communication with Wrigley Field. The Cubs and the St. Louis Cards were locked in a scoreless tie. Dizzy Dean was on the mound, Augie Galan at bat for the Cubs in the ninth inning.

Dutch saw the teletype operator start to type so he described the wind-up of the pitch. Then the wire went dead. Rather than announce to the public what had happened, he called it a foul ball. At least this wouldn't affect the outcome of the real game.

He looked expectantly at the window. Nothing was happening. Dutch decided to have Augie foul another one. He described in detail how a red-headed kid had scrambled through the rows to get the souvenir ball, how there had been an argument in the stands. Finally he had to get back to the pitcher.

For six minutes and forty-five seconds he had the batter hitting fouls. When the wire came back to life again, the news read Galan popped out on the first ball pitched.

"Not in my game he didn't," Reagan remembers. "He popped out after practically making a career of foul balls."

Dutch figures he covered in person at least forty-five football games from virtually every major press box in the Midwest, by telegraph more than six hundred big league baseball games, and the Drake relays, the nationally known track event.

He covered one swimming meet before it took place. Reagan was perched high on a diving tower with a microphone. He was to broadcast the outcome of four or five events of the National AAU championships for thirty minutes on a coast-to-coast hookup. Just as he was to go on the air, one of the AAU officials took time to discuss a few ruling changes with the participants. For thirty minutes Dutch described everything from the size of the swimmers to the color of the water. At the end of that time he turned the broadcast back to the station for other programming without having described a single event. Five minutes later the meet started.

Now that he felt secure in his job, his first thoughts were whether he could afford the ten percent of his income the family always gave to the church. His brother really needed that share to help himself through college. Reagan went to his minister and told him his problem. The minister agreed that giving ten dollars to a member of the family would indeed cancel out his obligation to the church for that year.

Moon graduated from college, but there was no job waiting for him. There seemed to be no prospects in Dixon. For want of a better thing to do, he visited his brother one week in Des Moines.

Moon went with Dutch to the studio on a Friday night because afterwards the two were going to join a group of friends from the station at a popular eatery and hangout, Si's Moonlight Inn. Dutch's Friday night program involved making a few predictions about the outcome of games coming up on the weekend. As he made them, he noticed that Moon was shaking his head in disagreement on a couple of guesses.

On a spur of the moment impulse Dutch turned on a mike in front of his brother and asked him his thoughts on a prediction. They continued to debate each subject, sometimes agreeing, sometimes not. Dutch promised to tell the audience the following Friday night who had had the best percentage of correct predictions.

The program director liked it. Moon was hired for a week to continue the dialogue. That job led Moon into other announcing work, to program directing , to network producing, and finally to the position of vice-president of a large advertising agency in California. Both the Reagan

Ronald Reagan
as a college student
at Eureka College.

*Wisconsin Center for Film
and Theater Research*

boys have come a long way from their small town beginnings.

Reagan had many friends at the station. One of them was Ernie Saunders. He was a reserve officer in the 14th Cavalry Regiment stationed in Des Moines. Through Ernie, Dutch learned anyone could sign up as a candidate and get a chance to ride in the cavalry.

It was probably because of all the Saturday-afternoon Westerns he'd seen in Dixon that this appealed to him. He wouldn't have to take a physical exam for a commission until he had completed preliminary training, which seemed a little strange. He was sure his eyesight would be against him, but in the meantime he could ride whenever he wanted.

For the next several months he took advantage of the army's excellent training in horsemanship. Finally the moment of truth came. If he wanted to ride anymore he'd have to face the army doctors.

He decided to go to a civilian doctor for a test that could be turned in on his record. He knew that if a nearsighted person punches a hole in a piece of cardboard, that pinhole will have almost the same effect as a corrective lens.

When the test came, instead of holding a black card over one eye, he used his hand. He managed to separate his fingers until there was a narrow slit. In reality he was reading the chart with his covered eye. He passed.

The only thing left was the final test in front of a platoon of regular-army cavalry. Two officers would be riding beside him and giving orders. The final obstacle was a huge jump made of telephone poles.

"I closed my eyes, grabbed a handful of mane, and landed on the other side of the jump a second lieutenant."

"There seems to be a part of me who always wanted to play cowboys and Indians," he admits, but one of his more heroic moments had a cops-and-robbers plot.

It was summer. His window was open. Suddenly he heard a young woman say, "That's all the money I have."

He looked out and saw a man poking a gun at her. Reagan, who liked target shooting for sport, had three guns in his room, but no ammunition. Still he grabbed an empty gun and pointed it out the window, shouting, "I have a forty-five in my hand, and I'm going to let you have it."

The would-be bandit fled. Reagan called down to the young woman that he would escort her home. "I was more frightened than she was," Reagan recalls.

Dutch Reagan had a popular following on the WHO wavelength. H.R. Gross of Iowa, who was the WHO's top newscaster and now is a Republican congressman, remembers that Dutch was often asked to speak before clubs and father-and-son banquets.

"He would tell sports stories, always adding some solid morality, urging his audience to stay away from drink, cigarettes, and cheating. He was a handsome, clean-cut young man who followed his own advice and was admired for it."

"I was doing pretty well in the sports announcing field," Dutch admits. The thought of acting had almost been forgotten, almost—until a series of events in 1937 brought it to the fore again.

Dutch Reagan was sent to Southern California to report on the Chicago Cubs' spring baseball training season at Catalina Island. That was the closest he'd ever come to Hollywood. It just so happened that a local Western band, which had been playing regularly on station WHO in Des Moines, had been signed to appear in a Gene Autry movie. Reagan went to see the band on the movie set.

Suddenly that dream of a theatrical career came alive again, and he started asking questions, "How do you get into this business?"

The band's agent arranged for Dutch to read for a casting director. The director was less than enthusiastic. Reagan had always had trouble reading a prepared script. He was better when the words came naturally from his own imagination. He hated to read commercials on radio. There was a stilted tone to his delivery. Yet when he'd had a chance to really get emotionally involved in a part onstage before an audience, he'd come through with a convincing performance. He told himself not to give up after just the first try.

While still in California, he looked up another friend from Iowa, Joy Hodges, a singer. She made two suggestions: first, that he remove his glasses when on camera, and second, that he get an agent. She introduced him to an agent, Bill Meiklejohn. Meiklejohn liked the looks of the broad-shouldered former athlete. He arranged for Reagan to take a screen test at Warner Brothers Studio.

Reagan was in front of the camera only a few minutes. He was told that the results of the test would not be known for several days. Where would they be able to reach him?

He was scheduled to return immediately to his radio job in Des Moines. If he stayed in California he might lose his only source of income. There wasn't much of a choice. He boarded the train for home.

Reagan recalls, "Actually I had done, through ignorance, the smartest thing it was possible to do. Hollywood just loves people who don't need Hollywood."

Exciting news was waiting for him when he got home. A telegram from his agent stated, "WARNER OFFERS CONTRACT SEVEN YEARS, ONE YEAR'S OPTION, STARTING AT $200 A WEEK. WHAT SHALL I DO?"

His answer was, "SIGN BEFORE THEY CHANGE THEIR MINDS." Reagan was walking on dream clouds.

Joy Hodges, who had made it all possible, wired the Des Moines *Register* and *Tribune* with the news. The story appeared in both papers.

His contract guaranteed him six months of work. The studio had the right to extend that option to as long as seven years, but they also could cancel any time after six months. He knew he might be back within the year, but not if he could help it.

At the end of May he headed for the West Coast in the "pride of his life," his first convertible. The first meeting he had with his new bosses was to pick his stage name. They had discarded "Dutch Reagan" as sounding too ethnic. Reagan had always thought Ronald too sissified, but when no other ideas were offered, they came back to the name Nelle Reagan had given him twenty-six years before. "Ronald Reagan" it was to be.

Four days after Reagan arrived in Hollywood he was starring in his first picture, *Love is on the Air.* There was no time for drama lessons and there was very little coaching. This was it.

Without any television competition Hollywood studios were turning out as many as 600 full-length productions a year. There were "A" pictures with superstars and generous budgets, and then there were "B" movies turned out in a hurry with very little money. This was where all young actors started.

The first day, they put him in front of a mirror and decided he needed no makeup. He had a healthy tan. This is something he can boast of to this day. Even as an older politician before a television camera, he has never resorted to makeup. In fact, he is allergic to it. "I can pass the white glove test any time," he's said. But there was one bit of advice from the "hair man." He'd have to let his crew cut grow out.

There were other bits of advice he had to pick up in a hurry. Close-ups were the hardest. He found out you had to avoid any sudden head movements. Even a slight swaying was exaggerated on film. He learned to find chalk marks on the floor without searching for them with his eyes. These marks positioned the actors precisely before the camera as planned by the director. And he learned that you don't come to a sudden stop when you hit those lines. If you do, it makes the actor look like a wooden soldier coming to attention. You have to shuffle your feet slightly to make the stop seem natural.

The second day he was on the set he saw the rushes, the prints of the film taken the day before. It was a shock. As Reagan explained it, an actor usually has a mental picture of the role he is playing. He projects himself into that role so thoroughly that it's a surprise to see himself on the screen from different angles. "You go to the rushes and somebody has stolen that heroic figure. There you are—just plain old everyday you—up on the screen. It's one hell of a letdown."

Contrary to stories about actors' jealousies, Reagan discovered that the cast was most often very willing to help a newcomer to the trade. Experienced performers were glad to pass along the tips they'd learned from others. Reagan kept his eyes open and took in all the lessons.

His first love scene was played opposite June Travis. Suddenly he found that there was more to a film kiss than a meeting of the lips. "I discovered that a kiss is only beautiful to the two people engaged in doing it. If you really kiss the girl it shoves her face out of shape. Your lips should barely meet and yet you must give the impression of a fervent kiss."

He suddenly realized that work was work and "kissing was more fun at a high school picnic."

His first publicity releases called him the new Robert Taylor, but it is to his credit that he didn't take the printed promotion copy sent out by the studios too seriously. He was in a business he liked and which was bringing him moderate luxury he and his family had never been able to afford before.

After his first movie he brought his parents to California. His father Jack had recently had a heart attack and was unable to work. Reagan kept him busy by giving him the job of handling the fan mail that had started to come in. Jack took charge of ordering the necessary photos and screening all mail to be answered. It gave him something to do.

Jack was happy, but he never tired of saying that Californians must be the hungriest people in the world. "There's nothing, by God, but real estate offices and hot dog stands."

Reagan bought his parents a small house, the first one the family had owned. He, himself, continued to live simply, in an apartment. He drove the convertible he'd bought in Iowa and owned exactly four suits. This was quite a problem in those days when actors furnished most of the clothes that they wore on camera. He had to juggle his appearances on screen to give the impression of an extended wardrobe.

It wasn't long before brother Neil arrived in California, but Moon continued in the field of broadcasting rather than following Ron into the movies.

The second picture that Reagan was in had been bought originally for Jimmy Cagney. When he turned it down, it found its way to the "B" unit. It was based on the true story of a cavalry horse that won the Grand National race in England. With Reagan's skill as a rider and his love of horses, it was a natural for him.

His next role he considered a step up in his career. He would be playing in a film called *Submarine D-1* starring Pat O'Brien, George Brent, and Wayne Morris, all established actors. His would be a small part introduced in the last reel of the film, but his name would be right up there with the "A" players.

Reagan learned a valuable lesson early in his career. Don't count on anything until the final film print is made. His part ended up on the cutting room floor, a disappointment he chalked up to experience.

But there were other action pictures, one after another, all low-budget films. He later said, "I became the Errol Flynn of the "B's". I was as brave as Errol but in a low-budget fashion."

He fought in a prison. He fought in a dirigible down at sea, and he fought in an airplane complete with trap door that could drop the villain from sight. Reagan was always cast as the wholesome, nice guy.

When it was learned that he could handle himself in fight scenes, they dispensed with doubles. He did whatever the director asked him to do. He swam through rapids. The bullets hitting the water six inches in front of his head were metal slugs from a sling shot. Any established star would have insisted that a stuntman take the risks, but Reagan obliged. Some of the pictures had great reviews, but there were some duds too.

He was a quick study, always knowing his lines, always conscientiously on time on the set. When a picture was to be shot in a period of days, not months, this was an asset a director didn't find very often.

During his first year in Hollywood Reagan played in seven pictures.

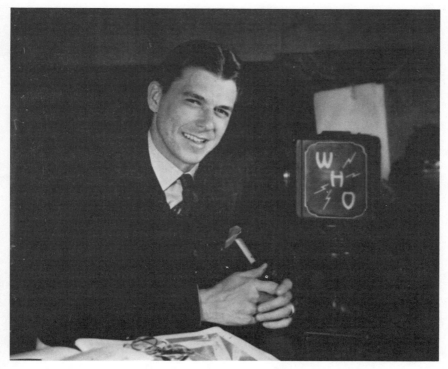

Ronald Reagan as a sports broadcaster for WHO Broadcasting Company.
WHO Broadcasting Company, Des Moines, Iowa

Reagan didn't exactly fit into the fast-paced life of the better-known stars. "He wasn't a night club kid," said Robert Taylor. "When I first met him, he was vitally interested in athletics and in keeping himself in great condition."

Reagan occasionally joined the social life of Hollywood, but for the most part it was planned carefully in advance by the publicity department. He was asked to escort a young woman named Lana Turner, who was under contract to the studio, to a movie premier. Reagan, in a borrowed dinner jacket, and Lana, in an evening gown from the wardrobe department, were both very nervous. Reagan was afraid to drive his old convertible, so he hired a taxi. He hadn't learned how easy it was to rent a limousine and act the part of star.

There was a special table at the studio commissary where all the stars ate. Everybody seemed to like Reagan, and he was taken into the "in" crowd.

"No formal invitation was issued. You just found you

were accepted," Reagan explained. Director Brick Enright sat at the end of the table. There was Mushy Callahan, studio physical education instructor and former boxing champion, and there were the names: Jimmy Cagney, Humphrey Bogart, Dick Powell, and Pat O'Brien.

There were wonderful stories to be heard from the lips of the very stars Reagan had always worshiped from afar. He heard Cagney tell about the Christmas dinner he and Pat O'Brien and Frank McHugh had in a cheap hotel room roasting hot dogs over an open gas jet because that was all they could afford.

There was also plenty of ribbing. The last one to sit down at the table became the target of the day. When it was Reagan's turn he was usually kidded about being a bona fide member of the horse cavalry, a sort of throwback to another generation.

Reagan took it all in good humor but probably felt more at ease making a speech at the San Fernando Y.M.C.A on clean sportsmanship, health rules, and the importance of team-play. He found time in his busy schedule to do this on many occasions.

The group he spent most time with was a gathering of old friends from Iowa who had come to California to make their fortune. Reagan was the only one for several months who had a job. He generously helped them out when finances hit the critical stages.

They explored California like all tourists, and they set up their own home-away-from-home at Barney's Beanery on Santa Monica Boulevard. Each boosted the other's morale. Today these friends have scattered. But there is a close feeling of camaraderie when paths cross.

One of the better pictures he played in during those early years was *Brother Rat*, a 1938 comedy about Virginia military cadets. There were three principal leads, Eddie Albert, Wayne Morris, and Reagan. Unhappily, Ron learned another lesson. There is room for only one star in a picture. It was Eddie Albert who had played the role on stage, who got the big break in that one. Reagan's performance was well received, but it wasn't a dramatic standout.

It was during the filming of *Brother Rat* that he met his first wife, actress Jane Wyman. They became engaged during a cross-country tour arranged by Louella Parsons, the Hollywood columnist. She had chosen a group of young actors and actresses she felt were headed for future stardom. A vaudeville act was put together, and they spent nine weeks together traveling from coast to coast.

A few months later in 1940 Ron and Jane were married in Hollywood with Reagan's parents looking on. The happy couple honeymooned in Palm Springs and moved into a Beverly Hills apartment.

Immediately their pictures were on the covers of the fan magazines. The captions read, "Ideal Hollywood Marriage." And for a while it seemed to be so, but there was little chance for privacy, at least if you wanted to further your career, and here there were two careers to consider.

Reagan's future seemed definitely to be on the upswing. He appeared in *Dark Victory* with Humphrey Bogart. It was a small part, but *Newsweek* magazine commented that he had turned in an excellent performance in a lesser role.

In *Hollywood Hotel* he played the part of a radio announcer. The star was Dick Powell. "I was one of the thousands who were drawn to this very kind man, who would think of him as a best friend. He always seemed to feel genuine pleasure at seeing you, and he had a way of greeting you with the line,'God love you.' He meant it."

About this time Reagan had an idea for a movie he tried to promote. He wanted the studio to make a picture of the life of Knute Rockne, one of the football's all-time great players and coaches.

It would also be the story of George Gipp. Gipp was an eccentric young man who had come to Notre Dame during Rockne's early days of coaching. He always dressed in a sweat shirt at a time when a sport coat was required for class.

As a freshman walking across the practice field, Gipp had picked up a rolling football and had kicked it back to the varsity players. He happened to kick it from one end of the field to the other.

Rockne suggested the young man put on a uniform and join the scrimmage. Because of his cocky attitude, Rockne put Gipp in the freshman backfield to carry the ball against the varsity team, thinking this would teach him a lesson when up against stiff competition. On the first play Gipp ran eighty yards for a touchdown. From then on he was the star of the Notre Dame team. He died two weeks after his last game. His spirit lived on for all the teams that followed.

Reagan was sure this true story would make an excellent, exciting movie, full of pathos and action. He talked to anyone at the studio who would listen. One day he read in *Variety* magazine that Warner Brothers was indeed planning on doing the story of Rockne with Pat O'Brien in the lead.

Reagan rushed to the office in exasperation, sputtering that this was exactly the picture he had been promoting, that no one had listened to his suggestion.

Brynie the producer-director, told him that they already had a writer for the project. Reagan explained that this wasn't at all what he had in mind. He wanted to play the part of George Gipp.

"We've already tested a dozen others for the part, and besides you don't look like a football player," was the answer.

Reagan agreed, as probably he didn't, dressed in his suit and necktie. He left the office and went back to his room. He rummaged through his scrapbook to find pictures of his college days as a football player. When he returned he slapped them down on the producer's desk. The producer looked at them with interest and asked if he could keep them for a while.

When Reagan got home he had a call that testing for George Gipp would be at eight o'clock the next day. When he showed up that morning for the test he was surprised and grateful to learn that the person playing the other part in the scene would be Pat O'Brien himself. Usually when a test is run, any contract player around is thrown into the action as a filler.

Reagan knew the part of Gipp by heart. He had lived it in his mind. The test scene was where Gipp is ordered to carry the ball at that first practice. He has to show the cocky brashness of the new recruit when he asks Rockne, "How far?"

Reagan won the part. It was only a one-reel section of the movie but, as he said, it was a nearly perfect part, "a great entrance, an action middle, and a death scene to finish up."

The premier of the Rockne picture was to be held at Notre Dame. Not only the whole cast of the movie, but other celebrities as well were going to make the trip. Two special cars had to be added to the Super Chief train. Nelle Reagan took Ron aside one day and told him that Jack wanted to go along. It was easily arranged, but Reagan was worried that there'd be plenty of temptation for heavy drinking.

Things went along smoothly until the partying started in South Bend. Ron called his father's room the day of the main event. There was no answer.

Some time later Reagan was told how the troop had returned to the hotel the night before. Jack had decided to protect them all from the mobs of autograph seekers he imagined were hiding in every alley. He would halt the group while he tiptoed to the next corner. After peering cautiously in every direction, he would signal them all to rush across the street for cover. There were whoops of laughter, and everyone seemed to enjoy the drama, Pat O'Brien most of all.

Ronald Reagan in the role of George Gipp in the film *Knute Rockne–All American*.

Wisconsin Center for Film and Theater Research

Ronald Reagan didn't think it was at all funny. In fact he held his breath wondering what would happen later in the day when the celebrations came to a climax.

Jack showed up sober enough to take his place at the luncheon table—right next to the mother superior of the Catholic girls' school nearby. Ron was not able to hear what was being said. He was even afraid to look in their direction, but on the way out of the dining hall the nun stopped Reagan to tell him that his father was one of the most charming men she'd ever met. From then on Ron stopped worrying about his father.

When Jack returned home, he told Nelle and Moon that he had had the most wonderful time of his life. He jokingly said he wouldn't mind if his heart did call it quits, now that he'd lived the life of a celebrity. Not long afterwards he suffered a fatal attack.

As a result of the good reviews Reagan had in that picture he was immediately put on call for the second lead in an Errol Flynn picture, *Santa Fe Trail*. Reagan was to play the part of young Lieutenant Custer, Flynn the role of J.E.B. Stuart, the great cavalry leader of the Confederacy. Raymond Massey had the role of John Brown.

Reagan had great admiration for Flynn but soon learned that the star lacked confidence in his own ability and continually tried to upstage the rest of the players. Time after time he'd have other players moved to the background of a scene or have them written out of the action altogether. Reagan realized what was happening.

In one scene he was told to stand behind a whole group

of soldiers. Reagan figured there was only one way he could still put himself in the picture. Quietly while they were adjusting camera frames, he started to scrape some loose dirt with his feet until he had a small pile to stand on. When the time came for his one line of dialogue, he had managed to put himself a few inches above the screen of people in front of him.

There were more lessons to be learned on how to hold his own with the pros. He wasn't considered a newcomer anymore. There were fewer helping hands. Reagan was delighted when he found out he was going to be loaned to MGM for the screening of the old Broadway play *The Badman.* Wallace Beery was the bad man, Lionel Barrymore was to be Reagan's crochety uncle, and Loraine Day was to be the love interest. Reagan was warned that he'd have his hands full trying to keep the others from stealing scenes.

Beery never rehearsed a scene the way he would say it on camera. That always kept the other actors on edge since they had to ad-lib their lines. Reagan's sports-announcing experience made him a pro at this, but he also had to contend with Barrymore's tricks before the camera. Lionel was confined to a wheelchair. He could swing it around on a dime.

Reagan remembers, "It's hard to smile in a scene when your foot has been run over and your shin is bleeding from a hubcap blow." And yet the cast completed their assignment on speaking terms, with good humor and respect for each other's talents.

Reagan played a concert pianist in *Million Dollar Baby*

and a string of pictures with the Dead End Kids, but his finest role was still ahead.

In *King's Row* he played the part of Drake McHugh, gay blade who dated all the girls in town. After being injured in an accident, he is cared for by Dr. Gordon, who disapproves of his attentions to his daughter. To get even, he amputates the young man's legs at the hips.

The big scene comes when McHugh wakes up in the hospital room and discovers what has happened to him. Reagan didn't know how he could possibly portray such a deep and terrifying emotion on the screen with no more than five words of dialogue. He consulted physicians and psychologists. He talked to people who were so disabled. He rehearsed the scene at home until he had worked himself into a pitch of panic. The night before they were going to shoot the scene he could not sleep at all.

The next day he wandered over to the set early. He saw that they had cut a hole in the mattress for his legs to hang through. He would be covered with a sheet and blanket. He climbed in the bed to see how it would feel. He stayed there for an hour, looking down at the flat part of the covers where his legs should have been. It began to terrify him almost as if he *had* lost his legs.

The director, Sam Woods, approached the set quietly. "Want to shoot it?" he said in a low voice.

"No rehearsal now?"

"Let's make it."

There were cries of "Lights!" and "Quiet please!" and then the call for "Action!" There was a sharp clack which signalled the beginning of the scene.

"Randy!" he screamed. Then he spoke the words that had been haunting him for weeks, "Where's the rest of me?"

Film had recorded the drama of the moment. There were no retakes. Everyone congratulated him, but it was minutes before he could snap back to reality.

Sneak previews proved that the picture was a smash success. Suddenly people began to realize that the wholesome, cheerful, rather square young man from the Midwest could act. Another way to measure the success of the film was a change in his contract. He was offered a salary three times more than he had been getting.

Before the film ever reached a theater he was called into the army. It was 1941.

Again he was required to take a physical. He passed with flying colors until it came to the eye test. The first doctor looked at his record and shook his head. "If we sent you overseas, you'd shoot a general."

A second doctor laughed and added, "Yes, and you'd miss him."

There were still plenty of jobs he could do. He first reported to Fort Mason in San Francisco where he was to be a liason officer organizing the loading of convoys. With his star status, he was also asked to attend bond rallies and help launch the newly created USO.

Reagan has often felt called upon to explain why he sat out the war in California. He was not searching for cushy jobs but was following orders, and those orders often gave him duty related to his acting experience. There were fourteen million Americans in uniform who didn't go overseas, but it was still something that he felt he had to apologize for.

Most of his assignments were directly related to the war effort, but one of his first duties was to help plan a program to boost morale at the post. A Presidential directive had been issued that each Army division observe an "I Am an American Day." Colonel Booker, who was in charge of Reagan's unit, worked out the details of the military parade, but the staging and casting of the rest of the program was up to Reagan. With his Hollywood connections, he was able to get Jeanette MacDonald to sing the national anthem. It was a stroke of genius. The officers and enlisted men alike felt their celebration was by far the most impressive.

Shortly afterwards he was assigned to the U.S. Army Air Corps. The Corps was setting up a motion picture unit that would produce training films and documentaries. The team they gathered together had been film cutters, camera men and propmen in the film industry before the war, and almost all were in the limited service category, either over age or physically ineligible for the draft.

The unit was called the 1st Motion Picture Unit of the Army Air Corps. They took over the Hal Roach studios, a nearby academy and an airfield. It was known affectionately as "Old Fort Wacky" or "Fort Roach," but they did a fantastic job of furthering the war effort.

There was a cloak of secrecy about their job. They were one of the few units outside the ranks of the strategic planners to know which targets overseas were marked for demolition.

A complete mock-up of Tokyo was built. It covered the

Ronald Reagan in uniform, with his mother.
Wisconsin Center for Film and Theater Research

entire floor space of a sound stage. The information came from all kinds of sources. Background pictures were collected from anybody who had recently traveled in Japan. Perhaps a botanist or a missionary had taken prewar pictures. Frequently a snapshot of a group of friends would reveal in the background just the right building they wanted.

A camera was rigged on a crane. The experts spliced in real film taken on flights over Tokyo. The final film print gave a realistic showing of the entire bomb run over the target. First the geography appeared as the pilot would see it. Then it would be shown as seen through a bombsight. The animation department gave a third view of the target as it would appear on radar if darkness or bad weather was encountered.

Those bomb runs were kept so authentic that they were continuously updated from actual film from reconnaisance planes. Burned out or bombed buildings immediately got the same treatment on the model.

One of Reagan's jobs was as commentator. His voice would come through with such lines as, "Gentlemen, you are approaching the coast of Honshu on a course of three hundred degrees. You are now twenty miles offshore. To your left, if you are on course, you should be able to see a narrow inlet."

His voice would talk the mission in until the words, "Bombs away," were given.

Propmen had even bigger jobs. Mockups were made of both enemy planes and our own planes to help the troops identify the differences from all angles, in flight. Also, all newsreel material of bombings and strafings for distribution to movie theaters throughout the country was put together in this studio from actual combat-film footage.

Reagan frequently was teased by some of the combat pilots who came in to advise on their projects, about being a member of the horse cavalry. At one time his regulation uniform had included the wearing of spurs. Reagan always turned it around with, "I was physically unfit for the cavalry but still plenty good enough for the Air Force."

There were thirteen hundred men and officers stationed at the base. Most had had no previous military training, but to keep up the military image there was regular drilling. Reagan was standing at the corner of a studio street one day when a column of marching men came swinging by. When a column approached, he came out in a stage whisper with, "Splendid body of men." With half as many I could conquer MGM." The ranks dissolved in laughter.

He was popular with his men. He never pulled rank or tried to avoid duty because of his prewar star status. Only once did he have an opportunity to play in front of a camera, not for his star salary, but for the $250 a month army pay.

Irving Berlin wrote and produced a musical comedy called *This is the Army*. Reagan played the lead opposite Joan Leslie. As Reagan described it, "George Murphy, who was later elected United States Senator from California, played my father. I've never let him forget it. We were close to the same age, and it took a lot of white dye on his hair to prepare him for the role."

Every bit of the profit from the film, more than ten million dollars, was turned over to the army relief fund by Warner Brothers.

Reagan was one of the lucky ones who could commute on weekends to his home nearby. A baby daughter was born to the Reagans in 1941. She was named Maureen. Again the screen magazines published pictures of the ideal Hollywood family. Reagan was thrilled to be a father, but there wasn't much time to enjoy his baby daughter.

Two years later Jane Wyman lost a second baby in childbirth. It was decided that they would adopt a son. As Reagan put it, "Michael came to us in 1945, closer than a son; he wasn't born unasked. We chose him."

The war was drawing to a close, and Reagan was anxious to get back to his career again. Before that was to happen he had to sit through hours at his desk unraveling government red tape. The army had ordered that every military installation reduce its number of civilian employees. However, many of their jobs were protected by civil service. Reagan watched the build up of paper work and red tape. He fought against it, but finally gave up. Those who were in the army and incompetent could not be fired without a trial similar to a military court-martial. He saw a self-serving bureaucracy at work. He would remember those days.

Reagan was on his way to the Disney Studios to narrate an animated short for the Signal Corps when he heard on the car radio that a bomb had just been dropped on Hiroshima. The account sounded more like a Hollywood script than reality.

The war was soon over. It was back to civilian life again. Somehow he had expected that the world would be a better place now. He was wrong. Another battle on the home front was about to start. It involved labor unions and movie studios and communists and right-wingers. Reagan found himself in the middle of it.

Reagan always had been very honest with himself in evaulating his screen career. During the showing of *King's Row* his popularity had been at its peak. Four years later the taste in Hollywood films had changed. The prewar generation of stars was going out of fashion. Now Hollywood was producing pictures with a social message. Audiences seemed to be obsessed with realism. The new stars wore undershirts and sweated and scratched on camera. There were new heros.

Reagan wasn't sure what the future would bring. He spent the first two months at home building a model boat, something he had never done before and has never done since. It was a time to contemplate his future. He was hoping to find a movie role that would reestablish his importance in the movie industry. Maybe he could change with the times.

While he was waiting for that big chance, he became increasingly involved with meetings of the Screen Actors Guild (SAG). This was an organization that had been founded in 1933. It was led by some very outstanding talent in the movie industry, name stars who were fighting for the little fellow, the bit players, the contract player, who could barely eke out a living on the fringes of the glamour industry.

Eddie Cantor described the SAG as getting its underlying strength from the backing of the big names who could bargain as they pleased. They could put real power behind "the little fellow who has never been protected and can't do anything about it."

When the SAG was first formed, ninety per cent of the actors got less than five thousand dollars a year salary, all this before deduction of the ten-percent agent's fee and taxes. Day players were in the majority, getting a day's pay of fifteen dollars perhaps once a week, if they were lucky.

A nine-day picture might stretch out for as many weeks. An actor would have to be on call and ready for work until the picture was finished, yet he would be paid for only the nine days he worked.

The main issues of the Guild were entirely related to job conditions. In no way was it connected with a political party. Ronald Reagan joined the Guild the first year he arrived in Hollywood. He had been persuaded to do so by a young actress, Helen Broderick, who saw the need to improve conditions. Reagan always had had a social conscience, that had been fostered by his parents back in Depression days. He quickly became active. He was appointed to the board of directors to fill a seat to represent the young contract players.The board was made up of all levels of performers. He was impressed to be working with famous stars and listening to their pleas for salary raises for extras of the lowest rank. All Reagan's doubts about joining such a union were dispelled after the first meeting. The Screen Actors Guild eventually became a member of the American Federation of Labor (A.F. of L.).

During the war years when Reagan had been absent, much had been happening. Two rival unions were locked in a struggle for control of the studio work force.

Most unions are set up where carpenters have their organization, plumbers theirs, and painters theirs. The International Alliance of Theatrical Employees (IATSE) wanted to give the stagehands the right to work at any of these jobs as he or she was needed. This was against the policy of the A.F. of L.

"A chair is a chair," the A.F. of L. union leader said. "It doesn't become a prop just because it is on a stage. Anything to be done with wood or a wood substitute belongs as a carpenter's job. A stagehand doesn't have a right to take a carpenter's job away from him."

Then there were arguments between the painters and the Screen Set Designers. The IATSE held to their argument, the craft unions to theirs. A strike was called. The Screen Actors Guild tried to get the two sides together to work out a compromise agreement. The cancellation of production was putting actors and everyone in Hollywood out of work.

There were fights when stagehands tried to cross picket lines. There were fights when labor organizers tried even to disrupt the planning of future movies.

The Guild asked a government mediation board to set up some kind of voting machinery so that the workers themselves could decide which union they wanted to join. It was a hectic time.

This was the situation when Ronald Reagan was discharged from the army. Almost immediately he was again appointed to the board of the Screen Actors Guild. He found himself in the middle of the battle. Every moment of his time was spent attending meetings and bargaining sessions. He traveled across the country to attend the A.F. of L. national convention and he was called to Washington to testify before the House Education and Labor Subcommittee.

He told them in Washington that, "it was about time we forgot all the rules and regulations and red tape and go back to the town-hall meeting idea, that the Guild take the lead and try to get the parties to sit down at a table in one room and hammer this out . . . instead of talking through newspapers. If we couldn't succeed, we would at least know which side or what individuals had failed to cooperate, which was more than we had been able to learn up till then."

Those meetings did bring a lot of truths to light, and some compromises were effected. There was still a lot of ugly fighting taking place. One union leader's home was bombed. Three painters who had crossed picket lines had their arms broken. Reagan himself received threats that if he didn't stop interfering with affairs that were none of his business, he'd have acid thrown in his face so that he'd never work as an actor again. His loyalty to the Screen Actors Guild never wavered, but he became more and more hostile to organized labor's national leadership.

The Reagans at home with their children Maureen (5½ years) and
Michael (15 months). The first Mrs. Reagan is Warner Bros. film
star Jane Wyman.

Wisconsin Center for Film and Theater Research

"About this time in my life," Reagan remembers, "I was blindly and busily joining every organization I could find that would guarantee to save the world. I bled for causes."

Reagan had followed his father's policial leanings by voting for the Democratic party in every election up to and including the 1948 victory of Harry S. Truman. His disillusionment with big government stemmed from some of his difficulties in working with bureaucracy during the war years. If his screen career was at an end, he would work with the tools he had—his thoughts, his speaking ability, and his reputation as an actor, to bring about some changes in government.

He became hell-bent on saving the world from neo-Fascism, people with attitudes similar to the dictators that Americans had fought against during World War II. He had not come to fear the Communist party yet. After all they had been our most recent allies. But as the warfare among representatives of labor continued, it appeared to some that much of the bitter feeling was being caused by a small group of agitators with known links to the Communist party.

A Senate fact-finding committee on un-American activities in California uncovered evidence that a considerable sum of money to finance such activities had come directly from the Soviet Union.

Testimony was also given by a former Communist member who had become disillusioned with the plot, that the Communists had set up a long-range plan which was to include three steps. First, they would line up big-name stars to collect money and create prestige without the stars ever knowing what cause they were supporting. Second, they would infiltrate the talent guilds and craft unions to gain control of executive positions. And third, (the reason for all this spurious activity) they would use the movies as a propaganda tool for the Communist party. The writers and directors were the ones who could do most to influence the content of movies produced.

When the Senate committee tried to question these writers and producers about their political beliefs, they refused. The Fifth Amendment to our Constitution gave them the right to remain silent so as not to incriminate themselves.

Reagan watched all of this happen. When the general membership of certain unions failed to attend meetings in large numbers, Communist sympathizers were there ready to take over, passing resolutions without debate to call strikes in the name of the entire organization. Many union officials found themselves voted out of leadership, their roles taken over by extreme leftist groups.

Suddenly America seemed to be heading toward extremes. Anyone tainted with a Communist label was condemned, blacklisted. Those who were, rightly or wrongly, given the label of Communist fought back, accusing their attackers of trying to deny them freedom of expression. Those who refused to sign statements that they were not—nor ever had been, members of the Communist party were "black listed"—meaning no one would hire them in the film industry.

Compared with others, Reagan was a moderate on the issue. *Life* magazine covered the Senate hearings. It said

"Ronald Reagan made his points neatly with a good deal of restraint and common sense."

In Reagan's own words, "The way to fight Communism is to improve America. The Reds know that if we can make America a decent living place for all our people, their cause is lost."

In a interview with a Hollywood columnist he said, "Our highest aim should be the cultivation of the freedom of the individual, for therein lies the highest dignity of man. Tyranny is tyranny whether it comes from right, left or center. It is evil."

And yet another quote shows his fear of the complacency of the American public in not fearing the left extremes. "Something the liberal will have to explain and stand trial for is his inability to see the Communist as he truly is and not some kind of Peck's Bad Boy of liberalism, who is basically all right but just a bit overboard and rough-edged."

Ronald Reagan served as president of the 15,000-member Screen Actors Guild for six terms. By his own admission he was spending five nights a week at the Guild office when he was not out of town. Eventually he was confronted with the possible breakup of his marriage. Jane Wyman stated flatly that she was bored with attending meetings herself and that her husband had no time for home or family.

Reagan did not want to see the marriage end, but he realized that there was truth to the charge. They once tried for a reconciliation, but by the summer of 1948 the divorce was final.

Reagan has never discussed the ending of his first marriage with the press. His only comment was that, "There is no easy way to break up a home, and I don't think there is any way to ease the bewildered pain of children at such times."

Jane Wyman was awarded custody of the children. Maureen was seven, Michael three.

A bachelor again, Reagan moved into an apartment. He turned to acting again.

President Reagan with his wife, Nancy, at the Inaugural Ball.
Michael Evans, The White House

Even during Reagan's most active involvement with the Screen Actors Guild he hadn't entirely left the movie screen. He played in the Hollywood adaption of the stage play *Voice of the Turtle*. He had argued against playing this role because it meant he had to give up a part in the film *Treasure of the Sierra Madre*. His preference was always for outdoor roles with a chance to ride, but he never dictated to the studio to get his way.

The movie version of *Voice of the Turtle* was not as smashing a hit as was the stage play. The movie he had had to give up turned out to be a film classic. It often seemed as if fate were stepping in to change his course of action.

He was at first pleased with his next assignment. He was to play the second lead with Humphrey Bogart in a film called *Stallion Road*. At the last minute Bogart was replaced by Zachary Scott, a fine actor, but not the drawing card to make the movie a box office success.

Yet the film had a lasting effect on Reagan. He fell in love, not with his leading lady, Alexis Smith, but with a horse.

Reagan was anxious to get back to riding and jumping

again, a sport he hadn't been able to enjoy during the service. He felt he needed a bit of coaching to perfect the riding skill he'd be expected to display on the screen. Nino Pepitone, a former Italian cavalry officer, was brought in to help.

Nino had also contracted to furnish one of his black thoroughbred mares, trained for jumping, for the part of Tarbaby in the picture. As Reagan put it, he got a case of "leading-lady-itis." He was not to be satisfied until he owned the horse. This was the beginning of the Reagan ranch.

Nino had a love of race horses. Reagan preferred the farm to the track. Between the two of them they worked out an arrangement where Reagan would buy some land and Nino would manage an operation. They would breed fine horses for pleasure riding and for racing.

Reagan searched the area and came up with an eight-acre plot of ground complete with stable and living quarters. Nino and his wife moved in, but Reagan did a lot of the work himself. His friends were amazed. He built a quarter-mile track with the inner rails slanted at the proper angle, and every post was dug by hand, his hands.

It was right after his divorce that he was sent to England to play in another war movie, *The Hasty Heart.* The setting was Burma as reproduced on a sound stage near London. Patricia Neal would have the feminine lead. A newcomer, Richard Todd, would play the difficult role of the Scotsman who is about to die.

It was Reagan's first trip abroad, but it came at just the

time he wanted to be working on his new ranch. It was a lonely four months. When he got back he had another stroke of bad luck. He was about to be starred in an exciting crime thriller with Ida Lupino, but on the Sunday preceding the starting date, he had a serious accident.

He was playing in a baseball game between comedians and leading men. Every year they held the event to benefit the City of Hope Hospital. Sliding into first base he broke his thigh bone in six places.

At the hospital the orthopedic surgeon decided that neither cast or traction would hold the leg together properly. Instead of a cast, he sheathed the leg with alternating layers of adhesive and sheepskin, embedding the sheepskin straps for traction between the layers of adhesive. The only problem was that he discovered he was allergic to sheepskin. For the first two weeks in the hospital his eyes were swollen shut. Later when they tried to give him antihistamines, he was so doped he couldn't stay awake.

As soon as he was off crutches he was back at work again. He played a Confederate cavalry officer in *The Last Outpost,* followed by a musical remake of *The Male Animal,* which they retitled *Working Her Way Through College.* Next came *Bedtime for Bonzo,* where, as a college professor experimenting with animals, he played second lead to a chimpanzee. There was no way to fight this scene stealer.

Reagan was still on call as president of the Screen Actors Guild. He had had no time for a social life. In the middle of Hollywood's Red scare, Reagan received a request from Director Mervyn LeRoy that he help a young MGM actress named Nancy Davis. She was afraid that radical leftist literature that was being delivered to her apartment might jeopardize her career. Those with even a hint of Communist leanings were still being blacklisted.

Reagan agreed to check into the problem. He discovered that there were two actresses in town with the same name. Apparently there had been a mix-up in identity. Reagan offered to telephone the news to the young lady, but LeRoy said the actress needed reassurance and suggested that Reagan and Davis meet over dinner.

Reagan was immediately on the defensive, sure that this was just another pretext of a young starlet wanting to be seen in public with a name actor. When he called, he told her it would have to be an early dinner because he had an early studio call in the morning.

She told him that was just what she had been hoping for, as she would have to make it an early evening too. As it turned out their early evening lasted until three the next morning.

Soon other dates were set up, but Reagan was in the midst of more bitter infighting between unions that were seeking to control live television performances and filmed programs for television. It was a new field for labor arbitration.

He had spoiled one marriage by working overtime. He was reticent about committing himself to another when he was just as busy.

Nancy Davis is a tiny brunette, always beautifully dressed in conservative expensive style, conservative for Hollywood, that is. Her stepfather was a nationally renowned surgeon, her mother a former Broadway actress. Nancy had been raised in a manner befitting a family of social prestige. She had attended a private preparatory school and had graduated from Smith College in the East, a far cry from Reagan's early years of near-poverty.

She had always been interested in acting and had appeared in summer stock and later in a Broadway play, *The Lute Song,* with Mary Martin and Yul Brynner.

She came to Hollywood, as she describes it, "not obsessed with becoming a movie star but because I didn't want to return to Chicago and lead the life of a post-deb." Almost immediately she was offered a contract at MGM and soon was playing in family-type melodramas, or "kitchen-cabinet epics," as they were called. Three pictures in a row she had to wear padded additions to her wardrobe as a pregnant about-to-be-mother. But she had held her own with Frederic March in scenes of *It's a Big Country.* She had talent.

Whenever Nancy and Ronnie, as she called him, could find time from their busy schedule they were together. Their friends took it for granted a wedding was in their future, but Ron had not proposed.

It wasn't until he was sitting around a large round table in the Producers Association meeting room one evening next to his good friend Bill Holden, that he made up his mind that all the business he had once thought so important was not making him happy.

Suddenly he picked up a scratch pad and wrote a note to Bill, "To hell with this, how would you like to be best man when I marry Nancy?"

Bill grinned, "It's about time." The two of them left the

meeting to make the proposal official.

There was still one more picture to be finished before the date was set. It was one that gave him pleasure and pride. *The Winning Team* was the life story of baseball's immortal Grover Cleveland Alexander. Nancy was as much a baseball buff as he was.

Reagan was coached by some of the best big league players of the day. Nancy came to the set to watch. He often tells the story that the best engagement present he gave her was a baseball autographed by the pros.

On March 4, 1952 they drove out in the San Fernando Valley to the "Little Brown Church." Bill and Ardis Holden were waiting for them. It was a simple yet beautiful ceremony. They returned to the Holden home for wedding cake and pictures, then headed for Phoenix, Arizona for their honeymoon.

Nancy's parents had a home in Phoenix, and although it may sound strange that they'd share such a private time of their lives with parents, Reagan recalls that it seemed very natural. He deeply admired Nancy's family, and some say that Dr. Davis, a wealthy and politically conservative man, had much to do with the later trends in Reagan's policies. However no one can deny that Reagan was heading in a conservative direction on his own.

Back in Hollywood, they moved into Nancy's apartment until they could find a home of their own. It was a strange time of commuting. Reagan still had his apartment, and they'd often dress for a party in their own separate quarters and meet somewhere in between.

They finally found a home they loved, with a view. It was in the Pacific Palisades area. Nancy immediately started decorating one room as a nursery. She was close to thirty, Ron just past forty. After playing so many pregnant roles on film, she was ready for the real-life experience.

She had never considered acting as a lifetime goal. It was something to do between college and marriage.

"If you try to make two careers work, one of them has to suffer," she said. "Maybe some women can do it, but not me."

Occasionally she did return to the studio for a film, but her family always came first. In 1956 she and Ron co-starred in *Hellcats of the Navy*.

Daughter Patricia Ann was born a year after their marriage. The baby came earlier than expected and with a few complications. She arrived by cesarean delivery.

Reagan was immediately overcome with pride and also the realization that he better get his career back onto a more even footing if he was going to provide for his new family. He resigned as president of the Screen Actors Guild to give himself more time for acting. However, no really good roles were offered, and he was afraid that any more mediocre ones would grind his career to a halt.

Ronald Reagan knew it is an unwritten rule of show business that you must never show need. "You are always flush and only interested in working for the love of the game."

For fourteen months he turned down all scripts that came his way. He sold the horse ranch and economized to make ends meet. There were a few guest spots on television and speaking engagements that he was paid for, but it was a rough time.

Reagan's agent finally came up with what Ron thought was an outlandish idea: an offer of a large sum of money to do a nightclub act in Las Vegas.

"You must be kidding," was Reagan's comment. "What would I do?"

The promoters pointed out that he had done dozens of benefit performances in his career, acting as master of ceremonies. They told him that's all he would have to do in Las Vegas. They would put a show together and Reagan would introduce the acts. They promised that, somewhere along the line they'd write in a part for the star of the show, Reagan.

What resulted was a smash success. Reagan played in a very funny sketch where he was dressed with a straw hat and a cane like a real song-and-dance man. One of the acts in the review was a male quartet. He did five minutes of fast patter, much of it unrehearsed, with the quartet, and he never quite had a chance to deliver the footwork. Everytime he started to dance they interrupted him. Reagan came on as a handsome, natural, unpretentious performer, something new for Las Vegas.

The show was a sellout every night. Other offers came in, but Nancy and Ron decided that two weeks of that kind of life away from their baby daughter was enough. The money had been good. It would just have to stretch a little further, until something else came along.

Something else did, which led him right into another career.

Ronald Reagan signing official documents.

Jack Kightlinger, The White House

Reagan had always been against performing in a television series, but Taft Schreiber, his agent, came up with a new twist to the idea. General Electric was in the market for a new show. The agency had put together a package calling for a weekly dramatic program featuring guest stars. Reagan would be appearing in no more than half a dozen of these plays, but he would be introducing all of them to the television audience.

What made the offer especially attractive was that the package included a number of personal appearance tours to GE plants across the country. He would be meeting employees and taking part in their extensive "Employee and Community Relations Program." Reagan had been chosen for the job because of his experience with the Screen Actors Guild. He was well known as a speaker and had done a great job promoting good public relations for the movie industry. He gladly accepted the job.

All the good things seemed to be happening at once. Again he was offered a part in a Western, that would be shot in the scenic area of Glacier National Park.

"It was like being paid for playing cowboy and Indian," Reagan admits. The picture was *Cattle Queen of Montana,* with Barbara Stanwyck, an actress he admired as a very fine pro.

In the fall The General Electric Theater aired the first performance of its eight-year run. Some of the plays were shot live on stage. This meant that all sets had to be built in a small space so the actors could rush from one to another as the action dictated. This method limited the plot of the dramas. Eventually the segments were shot as in the movies, cut and edited before appearing on the television screen.

All the shows were quality productions. The best writers were hired. Film stars were beginning to appreciate this new medium. With good scripts, these stars were begging for a chance to be seen on the GE Theater. It proved to be one of the most popular programs in the history of television.

The General Electric Company had 135 plants in forty states. Reagan visited every one of those plants and personally met the 250,000 employees. His talks were usually limited to twenty minutes in length, but sometimes there would be as many as fourteen groups he would be speaking to in one day.

Reagan tried to avoid giving a routine canned speech. It would have ruined the natural give and take of the audience. Reagan is best when he wings it without a text. Yet there was a certain pattern to his speeches.

He frequently referred to the battle he had just waged to keep the Communist party from taking over the movie industry. He again spoke of America's best defense: "We must make democracy work by ensuring everyone a vote and by keeping everyone informed. I believe that, as Thomas Jefferson put it, 'If all American people know all the facts they will never make a mistake!' "

He continued to state his philosophy that never should a political party be outlawed, but that individuals should never be gullible about promises given without analyzing them. "Only if the Communist party ceases to be a political agent and becomes a Soviet Union conspiracy should the law intervene."

His speeches were non-partisan as far as the two major political parties were concerned, although he frequently warned against centralized power in Washington doing away with freedom at the local level. "There is a danger that a permanent structure of government could grow so huge that it exerts power on the elected representatives and usurps their policy making functions."

Reagan's sincerity impressed many. Reagan's brother Neil was once asked what one single quality Reagan showed that made him a success in radio, films, and politics. Neil answered immediately, "Credibility as far as an audience is concerned. If you have that you don't have to worry about anything else."

Moon and Dutch were still close in spirit, although their paths did not cross very often. Reagan's schedules were dovetailed on a split-second basis. Along with the speeches, there was always picture taking. And, as he later recounted, "I drove a locomotive, revved up a jet engine, watched a plastic bottle receive a million volts of

X-ray, and fired a 20 mm. cannon so top secret I couldn't even tell Nancy about it. I enjoyed every whizzing minute of it."

In spite of the miles he covered, Reagan managed to be home a lot. His travel schedule was broken into segments of not more than three weeks at a time. When home he was a very private person. He and Nancy had close friends but rarely entertained in large groups. They cherished their family time, that frequently was measured, not in days or weeks, but months.

He now felt secure enough to make two property investments. In 1956 they built their dream house. It has three bedrooms, not huge by Hollywood standards. They are surrounded by the Santa Monica Mountains and on a clear day they can see Catalina Island. Nancy furnished it tastefully, and the General Electric Company made it a model of electric efficiency.

There was no place for horses though, so they went looking for pasture and paddock land nearby. They found an ideal spot, at least it was ideal for several years until a highway was cut through near the ranch. After that, land developers discovered the beauty of the spot. They held on to the ranch as long as they could afford to.

As Reagan explained it, "I wasn't buying land for speculation, but as soon as our property tax increased tenfold, I couldn't justify the cost of keeping the land as a recreation retreat."

He sold the acreage at a tremendous profit, but they were sad to give it up.

An extra room had been set aside in their dream house

President Reagan meets with Helmut Schmidt, Chancellor of West Germany.

Mary Anne Fackelman, The White House

for a second child. Reagan was worried, knowing that Nancy had not had an easy delivery with Patricia. But on May 20, 1958 Ronald Prescott Reagan arrived promptly and without fanfare. Robert Taylor and his wife Ursula, the Reagans' next- door neighbors, were at the hospital to offer congratulations. Little Ronnie, nicknamed "Skipper," became a very active member of the household.

In 1959 Reagan was asked one more time to take the presidency of the Screen Actors Guild. The Guild was trying to win for its members a share of the profits that studios were making selling post-1948 movies to television. The producers had rejected the Guild's demands, so all actors and actresses called a strike. It was the first strike in the Guild's history. Stars as well as bit players walked off the sets.

In the end, the producers granted the actors payments for the television sales of their old films, and part of the money was used for a pension fund. Reagan was one of those who drew up the documents.

Two reasons are given why The General Electric Theater was cancelled in 1962. The most obvious one is that after eight years the public was looking for something different. The other reason is that Reagan was becoming more and more political with his speeches. When the officials at GE asked him to limit his talks to their products, Reagan balked, "There just isn't all that much to say about an electric coffee pot."

It's to Reagan's credit that when The GE Theater was dropped from television in 1962, bookings had to be canceled for speaking engagements as far ahead as 1966.

He had found a popular following.

There was a two year lapse between jobs, but Reagan never wasted his time. He continued to raise money and give political support to candidates of his choice for the California legislature.

In 1964 Neil Reagan, now vice president of the McCann Erickson advertising agency, which handled the Borax account, suggested that his brother would be a natural to host *Death Valley Days*, a weekly dramatic show of the Old West. Reagan was hired for the same salary as he'd received from GE, but he did not have to travel. He was on the "twenty-mule team" show for two years, until his political career really got started.

In spite of the help he had given to the local Republican party, he had never held any official position on a national campaign. In 1964 the party was looking for an articulate spokesman for their conservative cause. Reagan accepted the post of state co-chairman of the Goldwater-Miller campaign.

Close to election time there was wrangling between the moderates and the right wingers. Enthusiasm for the ticket was low. Some of the influential state committeemen felt Reagan was the only person who could pull the party together. They raised enough money to pay for thirty minutes of television prime time and scheduled Ronald Reagan as the speaker. History was made that night, October 27, 1964.

The speech, "A Time for Choosing," was along the same lines as many he had been giving on the GE banquet circuit but it came at a moment for decision making, as he put it.

"You and I have a rendezvous with destiny. We will preserve for our children this, the last best hope for man on earth, or we will sentence them to take the last step into a thousand years of darkness."

This was a somber mood, but it brought conservatives rallying to the cause. The day after the speech, contributions started pouring into the Republican headquarters. Eight million dollars was tallied as a result of that one television appearance. For a brief moment there was a surge of hope that Goldwater could win the national election, but the rally had come too late. The Republican candidate for the United States presidency lost by an overwhelming vote. Most everyone thought that the conservative cause was lost forever.

A few who remembered Reagan's tremendous popularity started thinking two years ahead, to the California governor's election in 1966. Less than two months after Goldwater's defeat, a group of wealthy party members met to discuss the idea of Reagan as candidate. It was headed by A. C. Rubel, Holmes Tuttle, and Henry Salvatori.

Tuttle spoke their views. "I wouldn't give a damn how good looking a man was. . . or how good he could speak, if I thought his political philosophy and fundamental principles were contrary to mine, but this man has everything going for him. Reagan is the man who can enunciate our principles to the people."

When they approached Reagan, Reagan was not quite sure that he wanted to take the risk. Certainly the national landslide against his candidate Goldwater had proved that the country wasn't ready for his conservative ideas. He talked matters over with Nancy.

She remembers thinking that, "It would be a difficult

campaign. The Democrats had a pretty good machine put together."

Governor Pat Brown would be running for his third term. Reagan put off his decision. "If by August or September we feel there's overwhelming support for the Republican party, not just a primary, I'll do it."

When the time came, he was convinced that he had a chance, an uphill fight, but a promising one. "I believed in what I had been saying. I really wanted to prove that we could bring government back under the people's control."

There was a lot of opposition to Reagan. He had no political experience. He turned this to his advantage by saying, "This is the way the country was started, with citizens assuming the responsibility in government." He claimed he would represent the people more fairly as a citizen politician.

He was also criticized because of the support he received from the radically far-right John Birch Society. His answer was, "Any members of the society who support me will be buying my philosophy. I won't be buying theirs."

The race issue brought on more controversy. When Reagan had been campaigning for Goldwater, he had been quoted as saying he was against the Civil Rights Act as it was written in 1964. He answered, "I've spent my life opposing racism and bigotry. The record proves it."

Reagan's only serious opposition for the primary vote was George Christopher, a former mayor of San Francisco, but Christopher had lost two other state races. The Republicans of California were ready to go with a new man.

The Democrats made the mistake of not taking Reagan's candidacy seriously. Here, they thought, was just another movie actor, and "the movie industry is noted for its feather-brained people." They were sure he'd come up with some totally irresponsible statement that would prove his incompetence. That statement never came. Reagan had done his homework well. He also had some fine advice. A public relations firm put his platform together in neat, readable form, repeating his own words and then dramatizing them. They were calling his goal "A Creative Society." This appealed to the new population of middle-class conservative voters moving to the Golden State.

Everyone thought it would be a close election, but Reagan won by 993,739 votes. He became the thirty-third governor of California at fourteen minutes after midnight on January third, 1967.

The reason for the odd timing had nothing to do with astrological charts, as his enemies tried to intimate. It was just that Reagan was anxious to be sworn in at the very earliest moment it was legally possible. The former Governor had made a last-minute claim to power by appointing Democrats to a number of important positions from judges to clerks. Plans were changed suddenly to put Reagan in office immediately. This blocked some but not all of the appointments.

A small crowd gathered in the half-darkened capitol rotunda in Sacramento. Reagan was surprised to see that television cameras had been set up. United States Senator George Murphy, another former movie actor, led the procession to the platform. The oath of office was administered to Lieutenant Governor Robert Finch and to

Governor Ronald Reagan. It was a solemn occasion, but as Reagan stepped to the podium to make a few remarks, he couldn't help lightening the moment just a bit. "Well George, here we are on the late show again."

Speaking without notes, he pledged that his administration would attempt to follow the teachings of the Bible.

The next day he was in his office, ready to take over one of the most challenging jobs in the country. It was true that he had no experience in politics, and that his campaign had been run by hired people who then walked away and left it, but Reagan had made valuable friends over the years. He called upon them to help staff his organization as a team of experts. It was not always easy to find just the right person for the right job, yet some brilliant minds were assembled, and The Creative Society came into being.

"I came to this job never having sought it, never having believed that I should be in public office, and believing only that a set of circumstances had placed me here as a citizen with an opportunity to do something in behalf of the philosophy and ideas which I supported. I have told my cabinet and staff that we belong here only so long as we refer to government as 'they' and never think of government as 'we.' I made a pledge to myself that I would make every decision on the basis that I would never run for office again. I didn't mean that I wouldn't run, but I felt that the first time a man in public office makes a decision on the basis of what it might or might not do with regard to votes in the next election, he has begun the path of compromise from which there is no turning back."

The President presides at a Cabinet meeting.

Michael Evans, The White House

Reagan had to deal with a budget deficit of about a quarter of a billion dollars, plus a state debt from the previous year. He had pledged to cut taxes and change the spending philosophy from the past. Where was he to start?

The Berkeley campus of the University of California had been the scene of some wild demonstrations by radicals during the 60's. University President Clark Kerr had been trying to keep order but it was a monumental task. He was quoted as saying, "The University is not engaged in making ideas safe for students; it is engaged in making students safe for ideas."

One of Reagan's campaign promises was that he would "clean up the mess on campus." A commission was set up to study the complete breakdown of order on campus. Certainly many, many students had nothing to do with the demonstrations, and it was well known that some of the most militant agitators were not enrolled at the University, but the only solution seemed to be the appointment of a new administrator. The Board of Regents, with Reagan's blessing, voted to remove Kerr. President Kerr felt he was being unduly blamed for the student unrest that really was a national, not a local, protest.

Reagan's controversial role at the University was not over. He had promised to cut spending. Looking at the $1.7 billion allocated for education, this seemed like a logical place to start. First, the budget would have to be slashed. Second, he planned to make up some of the deficit by an unpopular course, charging tuition for both resident students and non-residents of California.

This went against all previous principles of free education of which Californians were proud. Suddenly Reagan was a villain. The Speaker of the Assembly, Democrat Jessie Unruh, said, "The Governor is replacing The Creative Society with an illiterate society. The budget proposals are designed to punish dissent."

Reagan answered, "Observe the rules or get out. Higher education in our state colleges and universities is not a right, it is a privilege."

Reagan had been urging that the Board of Regents put the matter to a vote. The Regents did not want to oppose the new governor, but they did not want to do away with the free education program.

"We must solve the problem, so that we can get on with the business at hand, the selection of a new president," Reagan urged.

The Regents, backed into a corner, had no choice. They had to stand up and be counted. They voted 14-7 against the tuition proposal.

Immediately Reagan called a luncheon recess. His words to his staff were, "You never leave the stadium at the half."

The debate continued around the cafeteria table. Chancellor Murphy (head of the entire state university system) said that he most feared a continued escalation of tuition charges.

"What are the alternatives?" asked Reagan. The discussion continued long past dessert.

A final plan was drafted which eliminated the word "tuition." The new plan called for "a charge of two hundred dollars. . . to finance a program of student aid, faculty enrichment and/or other uses to be determined by the Regents."

Jessie Unruh, who had led the fight against tuition, thought he had won. When the meeting reassembled he realized he was facing a very smart "non-politician."

Ronald Reagan had promised to cut taxes and government spending. His opponents argued that the state debt had increased since Reagan had taken over as governor. Actually total expenses had increased, but so had the population of the state. Government spending per person was down.

Some of the services to the public were eliminated. Welfare relief was cut—an unpopular move—but the ever-mounting burden of debt had at least been halted, and there was hope for a balanced budget.

While Ronald Reagan was having his difficulties with the budget, Nancy Reagan was having her problems settling into the governor's mansion. It was a depressing and deteriorating heap of Victorian-Gothic gingerbread. It was located on a one way street that funneled heavy traffic through the city. When trucks passed, the windows rattled. What was more worrisome, it was a firetrap. Patti was away at school most of the time, but for Skipper, with no friends close by, it was more of a prison.

Finally the family decided to rent a home in a residential section of East Sacramento. Reagan's friends tried to raise funds for a new home for California's governors, but with Reagan's austerity plan, this didn't seem appropriate at the moment.

The family move brought about harsh comments. Wasn't the Governor's mansion good enough for the Reagans? Was the Governor trying to shut himself away from his job? Another hard lesson was learned. Anyone in the political spotlight is target for criticism. You live with it and do the best you can. It was easier for Ron than Nancy.

Their home life settled into a routine that would have surprised many. Often Reagan arrived home by six, showered, changed into pajamas, and settled down to watch television. This brought about complaints that he was a part-time governor. You couldn't run the state on a nine-to-five time schedule.

Actually Reagan worked out a system to deal with his monumental job. He recruited large task forces of experts to study specific problems. His staff collected and distilled those facts and turned them into concise reports. Although

---

President Reagan is shown with Margaret Thatcher, Prime Minister of Great Britain.

Jack Kightlinger, The White House

it was Reagan who set general directions and made the major decisions, the policy coordination and execution was frequently left to his aides. Although he certainly wasn't accomplishing all that he had set out to do, the system seemed to be working.

Reagan's backers had even bigger ideas for him: today the governorship, tomorrow the presidency. Why not? There were still plenty of conservatives around. Not all were bank presidents. Southern Democrats as a whole swung to the right more than many Republicans. Washington correspondent Baxter Omohundro wrote, "Reagan is the biggest thing to come along since corn pone and hog jowls."

A "Reagan for President" committee was put together before Reagan ever gave approval to the idea. He denied having his eye on the White House, yet he answered the call for any and all cross-country speaking tours.

As a non-candidate, he waited to see who might be in the running. There was talk of Percy from Illinois and Rockefeller of New York, but as time grew near, he could see that Nixon had taken the lead. Yet Reagan permitted his name to be placed in nomination as favorite son from the State of California.

When the final tally showed that Nixon had won the required number of votes for nomination, Reagan rushed to the podium to urge the convention to "declare itself unanimously and unitedly behind the candidate Richard Nixon as next President of the United States."

That was not the last time Ronald Reagan would be standing on the platform at a national convention. He was building to the future.

Knowing that the years at Sacramento would soon be over, the Reagans started talking about finding a small ranch where they could get away a few days at a time from the public life they had come to expect. Ranch life was Reagan's way to unwind. "Everything looks different from the back of a horse," he said. What they were searching for was "less a farm than a chunk of wilderness."

One weekend when they were visiting their friends Betty and Bill Wilson at their place north of Santa Barbara, Bill suggested that there was some land he thought the Reagans should see. They started up a narrow mountain road with one switchback after another. Seven miles further they turned off on a gravel lane through a forest of live oak.

Suddenly they were looking down across a sloping meadow toward a cluster of farm buildings. To the west of them was a sweeping view of the ocean, to the east the Santa Ynez Valley viewed from a saddle ridge 2,400 feet up in the Santa Ynez Mountains.

The main house was a ninety-year-old adobe building.

There were no questions. They had found their ranch. When the papers were signed, they started to work immediately to make it their own. With only limited help, they put in a lawn, an orchard, and a garden. Corral fences had to be built, but instead of the whitewashed Kentucky-style fencing they'd had on their other property, they achieved a more rustic effect here by using old telephone poles, notched and fitted against short upright posts.

There is even a small lake on the land, complete with a canoe. Instead of breeding horses, they turned to raising cattle in a small way. They keep them through the grazing season, then sell them off and start with a new herd the next year. They have their own favorite riding horses, of course. Ron long ago taught Nancy and the children to share his love of riding.

They were not too reluctant to leave Sacramento. Now there'd be more time for the ranch, at least that was their first thought.

The day they packed the last of their belongings, the state employees in the governor's office gave the Reagans a California landscape painting. "It means a great deal more to us than just a work of art," Nancy explains. "It reminds us of a very wonderful part of our lives."

The Reagans will be remembered there too. When the last of the books from Skipper's room were packed in boxes, there at the back of one of the shelves, appeared a neatly printed sign: "Ronnie Reagan slept here."

It was not a time of retirement for Reagan. He started to write a newspaper column. He also broadcast a daily radio commentary and gave speeches across the country.

In 1972 Reagan was asked to give the keynote address at the Republican National Convention, which was held in Miami Beach, Florida. He also was scheduled to chair the convention until a permanent presiding officer would take over.

There was talk of Reagan being put on the ticket with Nixon, but political advisers felt the wave of conservative appeal had vanished with Goldwater. Nelson Rockefeller was thought to be the favorite to run as vice president. The ticket selected was Richard Nixon and Spiro Agnew. In the final election the Republicans were able to defeat Democrats George McGovern and Sargent Shriver.

Ronald Reagan started planning for the 1976 election year. "This time I won't be a reluctant candidate. I'll run like hell," he said.

He was up against all the same prejudices he'd run into when nominated for governor of California. Everyone seemed to like him except the politicians. The standard joke was, "Ronnie for president? No, Jimmy Stewart for president. Ronnie for best friend." He was called, "Mr. Clean, too corny to be true."

Over the years he's learned how to take the jibes. "Politicians are a breed apart. They say pretty dastardly things about you, yet have dinner with you the next night and don't think you should pay any attention to it," he said.

His speaking engagements kept him in the eye of the public. His greatest support came from the grass roots. As one writer put it, "No one wanted him but the people."

Whenever he came through with the familiar phrase, "A

government agency is the nearest thing to eternal life we'll ever see on this earth," applause was mixed with laughter. He knew how to combine a folksy sort of humor with the serious message he wanted to get across.

He was ready for the 1976 convention. The Republicans had lived through the Watergate scandal. Gerald Ford had salvaged some of the integrity of the party, but many felt that he had been too involved with the disgraced administration to be accepted by the people.

Reagan and his campaign manager John Sears came to the convention with the intention of pushing through a change in voting procedure. In the past no one running for president had announced his choice for vice-president. Reagan felt that the vice-presidential nominee was equally important to the success of the ticket and that the convention delegates had a right to know that name. With Republicans split into right and left wingers, politicians were trying to come up with a compromise ticket. Reagan wanted to compel Ford to name his running mate before Ford's own name was put to a vote.

Reagan's forces lost the decision. Reagan was the only one who announced his choice for vice-president. He selected Senator Richard Schweiker of Pennsylvania. Schweiker's views were considered a lot more liberal than Reagan's. This brought cries that Reagan himself was playing politics, weakening his position as leader of the conservatives.

Ford won the nomination and picked Robert Dole of Kansas for the second position on the ticket, but it was the previously unknown Jimmy Carter who carried the

The President phones from the Oval Office.
Bill Fitz-Patrick, The White House

election, for the Democrats in 1976.

The morning after the election, Reagan was asked how he felt after another defeat. He spoke with confidence, saying he felt that his efforts had not really been futile. The Republican platform incorporated many of his ideas. Then he quoted from an old Scottish ballad. "I'm hurt, but I'm not slain. I'll lie me down and rest a bit and then I'll fight again."

Each defeat seemed to make him stronger. He was a national figure to be reckoned with. But there was now a time for resting, a time for the Reagans to be by themselves. The children had grown up and had lives of their own. Maureen and Mike had helped their father campaign. Although all of the members of the family did not fit into an intimate relationship, they respected each other and, as Maureen said, "really have been closer to Dad than during childhood." Patricia was the shy one who stayed out of the limelight as much as possible.

Skipper, now called "Ron," had entered Yale University. Earlier, when he was attending Webb School in Claremont, California, he had received a thoughtful letter from his father. This letter also tells us much about how Reagan views his own life.

"Here again what you do now affects the choices you have. When I was announcing sports I was happy and thought that was all I wanted out of life. Then came the chance at Hollywood, and that was even better. Now I'm doing something that makes everything else I've done seem dull as dishwater when I look back. But without some of the things I had to learn in college and didn't particularly care about, without some of the chores I didn't like when I was doing the GE television show, I couldn't and wouldn't have had the chance to do what I'm doing now.

"We don't know what turns our life will take or what doors will open, and there is nothing worse than to have such a door open and then learn you gave away your admittance ticket back in your school days."

Often there were family gatherings at the ranch. It was always a place to go to regenerate flagging enthusiasm. There was still much to fight for. The nation's economy was in a spiraling cycle of inflation. As Reagan put it, "We face a disintegrating economy, a weakening defense, and an energy policy based on the sharing of scarcity."

Reagan's ideas about cutting government spending were gathering more followers. Drastic measures were needed. The sentiment seemed to be, "This time we have the right man at the right time."

Reagan proposed large tax cuts, hoping to stimulate the economy and raise the productivity level of manufacturers and farmers throughout the country. If these companies and individuals did not have to give so much of their income to the government, they could spend surplus funds on growth, on enlarging or improving their operations. With an increase in the supply of goods, inflation would be halted.

At the same time the government would have to cut back on spending drastically to balance the budget. Many politicians were upset at the thought of doing away with special projects and increased welfare spending, but Reagan felt that if the country continued with its spiraling inflation no one would gain. There would be more unemployment as more and more businesses failed.

The only part of the budget Reagan was willing to see increased was for military spending. He felt that the defenses of the country had been sorely neglected and that to keep pace with the Russians we would have to develop new weapons and increase our supply of old ones.

These were the main issues he campaigned for against the other Republicans in the primaries. The top contenders seemed to be George Bush, Howard Baker, John Connally, Philip Crane, and Robert Dole.

The 1980 Republican national convention was held in Detroit. Reagan and his family sat in their hotel room watching the nominating speeches. It seemed like a replay of events before, but this time Reagan was not the underdog.

When it came to the roll call, Montana's twenty votes pushed Reagan's total above the 998 needed. It was then time to leave for the convention hall to make his acceptance speech. Yes, he'd been expecting the victory.

The podium was painted blue with white lettering: "Together—A New Beginning." When Reagan appeared, the crowd went wild. Horns blew, people chanted. Some 1200 red, white, and blue balloons floated from the ceiling, some landing on the bank of red and white carnations by the speaker's platform.

The speech was a pledge of change. Reagan quoted Thomas Paine, "We have it in our power to begin the

world over again." He believed it. Would he be able to accomplish it?

There was more cheering, but he knew it would be harder to evoke such enthusiasm from a bipartisan crowd. His work was cut out for him and he planned to keep that promise and "run like hell."

An election victory depended on how well he could appeal to the blue-collar worker and to the moderates throughout the country. He not only had to fight against Jimmy Carter, but also he had to oppose a third candidate, John B. Anderson, who had broken away from the Republican party when his own ideas had been dropped from the party platform.

There were two rules Reagan set for himself. "Thou shalt not be overconfident, and thou shalt not criticize other Republicans." Without unity in the party the Republicans could not hope to win against the Democrats who outnumbered them in all parts of the country.

A television debate between Carter and Reagan was scheduled for October twenty-eighth. Thousands of people would be watching. The polls still showed an outstanding number of uncommitted voters.

Reagan spent hours going over reports and statistics and watching video tapes of his opponent so that he would be well versed on any topic President Carter brought up. To help him rehearse, he chose one of his staff members to be a stand-in for Carter. Relentlessly this man threw questions

---

The President of the United States.

Michael Evans, The White House

to him, challenging his stand on every issue.

Carter was doing the same thing at Camp David.

When the day of the debate came, both men appeared assured and ready, but there was a tenseness to the scene. So much was at stake. For ninety minutes they debated the future of the country.

Some said Carter led on debating points, Reagan on style, but the only vote that counted was the one to be held on election day. They'd have to wait for November fourth.

As the reports of local polling tallies arrived at the national-television-broadcasting command posts, it became evident that it was not going to be the close election that the experts had predicted. Reagan won by a landslide. The popular vote showed 51% for Reagan, 41% for Carter, but in the electoral vote by states, Ronald Reagan won by the outstanding margin of 483-49. At sixty-nine years of age Ronald Reagan became the fortieth president of the United States.

The inauguration was not the prime news on television January 20. It was also the day the American hostages were released from Iran. But for Ronald Reagan it was truly a day of new beginning as he took the oath of office.

The grandstand was set up on the west side of the Capitol, with the dramatic view of the mall and the Washington monument to the front. Chief Justice Warren Burger presided. Ronald Reagan swore "to preserve, protect, and defend the Constitution."

The Marine band played "America the Beautiful" and

later "Hail to the Chief." There were parades and parties and celebration, but the next day Ronald Reagan settled into the Oval Office to try to put into practice the ideas he had been promoting. It was not to be an easy job.

Balancing the federal budget was Reagan's number-one priority. David Stockman, a young man with textbook plans, was appointed director of the Office of Management and Budget. During the time of his confirmation, he told senators and congressmen, "If we fail to cut taxes we have no chance, no hope, of bringing the budget into balance. The single problem today we have to address is utter lack of confidence that the government can get control of its budget and the Federal Reserve can control the money supply sufficiently to bring down inflation."

These were the same views as the man who had appointed him, the President. Together they set about convincing the public that only by reducing the size of government and stimulating productivity in private business could inflation be curbed and healthy economic growth fostered. The one area of big spending the President was unwilling to cut was the military budget.

Cutting federal spending meant shrinking some social programs. There were cries that Reagan would cause increased hardships for the poor while giving tax advantages to the wealthy. Reagan insisted that if the economy were left to adjust to his new rules, employment would increase and prosperity would return. Success could not be guaranteed without stopping the runaway accumulation of the nation's debt.

Congressmen agreed to the President's plan if their personal priorities were left untouched. Representatives from agricultural states were in favor of slashing urban renewal programs if farm supports were left intact. City mayors were arguing that if responsibilities for public programs were referred to state and local governments, they had to have a bigger share of tax dollars to provide health benefits, education, and law and order for their citizens. Farming areas with much smaller populations would have to share the cost.

Reagan traveled across the country, speaking before large audiences and appearing on television. And he was skillful at winning legislators to his way of thinking in personal chats.

Stockman was a fine ally, although later he published memoirs critical of the administration. He had an unprecedented mastery of the details of the federal budget. He was often able to overwhelm his opposition in Congress with a relentless recitation of dollars and cents figures. In the words of one Washington analyst, "Stockman demonstrated that knowledge was clout."

Political analysts have pointed out that Ronald Reagan's conservative ideas changed the direction of American government more dramatically than any other president in half a century. He slowed, if not reversed, the trend toward centralized government that had begun with the New Deal and Franklin Delano Roosevelt.

He's a man who admittedly would like the future to turn back to the past when a simplified work ethic could solve world economic woes, when government was a fourth cousin several times removed rather than a big brother legislating controls in many areas of private life. Yet Reagan knew that much of that legislation came about to heal the pains of the Great Depression. There is no way to set the time clock back, but he has stated that if federal deficits keep increasing at the present rate, he is certain a financial panic will follow.

Reagan's complaint is voiced as a question. Can future generations afford to pay for what the present government has promised them? Will there be enough money in the treasury to finance the needs of the elderly and sick and dependents in the next decade? And what will those dollars buy?

But on March 30, 1981, all the news of budget proposals was relegated to the back pages of the nation's newspapers. Headlines screamed, "PRESIDENT SHOT!"

About 2:30 P.M. the President had emerged from a side entrance to the Washington Hilton Hotel where he had just delivered a speech to labor leaders. He smiled and waved to a small crowd as he approached his limousine. Reporters and TV cameras were grouped behind a rope barricade about twenty feet away. One of the reporters shouted, "Mr. President, Mr. President," hoping for some comments to the press.

Suddenly a shot, like the popping of a firecracker, sounded—then a series of shots, all coming from the direction where the reporters were standing, were heard.

President Reagan is shot.

The President "just sort of stood there, then the smile sort of washed from his face," the reporter who had called out said later.

A Secret Service agent brusquely pushed Reagan into the limousine, which drove away immediately. In the meantime, security officers were swarming over a young man who a minute before had been holding a gun. Three bodies sprawled on the sidewalk. A pool of blood slowly seeped from the head of James S. Brady, the President's press secretary. Secret Service Agent Timothy McCarthy and Thomas Delahanty of the Washington police department had also been hit. Ambulances were on the way.

Within minutes the news was on nationwide television. Pictures of the President the moment he was hit were replayed every hour. People waited anxiously to hear the latest hospital reports. The President was undergoing surgery to remove the bullet that had entered his left side.

Secretary of State Alexander Haig announced that he was taking charge until Vice President Bush, who was in Texas for a speaking engagement, returned. Actually the Constitutional order of command stipulated that the Speaker of the House was the one to assume the responsibility, but few had bothered to look up the law.

It soon became apparent that President Reagan would not be out of commission for long. He had even started joking with the doctors. "Please tell me you are all Republicans," he said. The next day when top aides gathered at the hospital, he grinned when he asked, "Who's minding the store?"

The man who had fired the shot was not some crazed revolutionary, but a love-sick college dropout with a background of mental illness. He had been trying to impress a young Hollywood star with his irrational act. His name was John Warnock Hinckley, Jr.

In spite of his age, seventy, Reagan's recovery was remarkable. He was conducting business from his hospital room the next day, and within less than two weeks he was back at the White House.

The world around him was suffering violence as well. On May 25 Pope John Paul II was shot, and on October 19 President Anwar Sadat of Egypt was shot and killed by assassins. The world was shocked, but there seemed no way to stem the wave of terror.

In July of 1981 Reagan attended his first summit conference, hosted by the Canadian government. The heads of state òf Great Britain, France, Italy, West Germany, and Japan as well as the United States were present. No significant changes in world policies followed the conference, but it gave the leaders of the Free World a chance to exchange ideas and to promise cooperation.

"We leave with a true sense of common understanding and common purpose," said President Reagan.

Prime Minister Pierre Trudeau of Canada said the talks had strengthened "mutual trust and confidence in facing the crises that challenge us."

Back in the nation's capital, Reagan announced that he had proposed the name of Sandra Day O'Connor to fill a vacancy on the Supreme Court, which had come about when Justice Potter Stewart resigned. The appointment was applauded by almost everybody. Justice O'Connor was to be the first woman to serve on this, the highest court of the land. She was well qualified, but her few critics felt that she might be too conservative. Being by far the youngest member of the Court, her influence would be felt for many years to come.

It was also noted that if Reagan served a second term as President, he might be called upon to fill other vacancies. He would surely choose qualified lawyers who shared his own political views. That was a possibility, but of course there is no way to know how a justice will vote on any one question.

Justice O'Connor has frequently been seen as a middle-of-the-roader. She has often voted to uphold the verdicts

Justice Sandra Day O'Connor and her husband have lunch with the President.

AP/Wide World Photos

of lower courts, feeling that states have the right to interpret their own laws. She has tended to side with decisions strengthening law-enforcement rules, yet she has not led the fight for women's rights as many had hoped she would.

Reagan has been forced to take sides in many controversial issues. Personally he is against abortion, which angers some women's groups. He has also been severely criticized by some Jewish groups in the United States for selling military planes to Saudi Arabia. The planes are equipped with sophisticated radar to warn of approaching enemy attacks. Reagan's own concern was that a balance of power be maintained in the Middle East to encourage peace.

However, peace has always been hard to maintain in that part of the world. United States troops were called upon to police an area in Lebanon where there had been fighting between Moslem and Israeli forces. There were bound to be casualties. Critics lectured that we were entering another undeclared war that could never be won.

Such criticism reached a climax on April 18, 1982, when a car skirted past the sentry gate at the U.S. Embassy in Beirut and rammed its way across the sidewalk to the front entrance of the building. Immediately there was a flash of fire, and the entire building began to sag in a cloud of dust, splintered glass, and twisted steel. Forty-seven people were killed, seventeen Americans. More than a hundred were hospitalized. U.S. Ambassador Robert Dillon narrowly escaped injury, but other top members of the diplomatic corps were among the dead.

Reagan fiercely denounced the attack as a "cowardly act," but how was America to fight back? The government of Lebanon denied having anything to do with such extremists. People remembered Reagan's criticism of the way the Carter administration had handled the terrorists in Iran, but here there was no head of state to blame, no representatives of a government to deal with.

Six months later another attack occurred. Shortly after dawn on October 23 a TNT-laden truck crashed into the Marine compound at the Beirut airport, blowing up a headquarters building filled with sleeping U.S. troops. Almost simultaneously a second truck blew up a French paratroop barracks two miles away. Both buildings were reduced to rubble. The Marine death toll of 200 far exceeded that incurred in any single action of the Vietnam War.

Again the President expressed outrage and declared that the United States should be "more determined than ever" that the forces behind the ruthless attack "cannot take over that vital and strategic area of the earth."

Rescue workers clear debris after bombing of Marine Command Center, Beirut.

AP/Wide World Photos

However, the sentiment at home was that American troops be withdrawn. We were expanding our sphere of influence too far and had not accomplished the peaceful goal we had attempted. Gradually, U.S. forces were removed, yet a show of naval power kept a certain tense calm in the Middle East the following year.

On the other side of the world in Central America the United States was harassed by threats of Communist take-overs in the countries of El Salvador and Nicaragua. Help in the form of weapons was sent to those fighting for a freer form of government. Ambassador to the United Nations for the United States at the time, Jeane Kirkpatrick, said she saw no inconsistency in Washington's support of the rebels in Nicaragua and the government in El Salvador. "We are backing people who share our democratic and humanitarian concern for life against repression."

On October 25, 1982, Reagan surprised the world by sending American troops into Grenada. The President announced that the United States had received an "urgent, formal request from the Organization of Eastern Caribbean States (OECS) to restore law and order in Grenada."

The landing had been necessary after "a brutal group of leftist thugs" violently seized power and killed the prime minister of the country, Maurice Bishop. Reagan and his administration were concerned about protecting the lives of some 1,100 U.S. citizens in Grenada.

The United States had long been nervous about the stability of Grenada. Satellite pictures showed a large military buildup at one end of the island. A 10,000-foot runway for planes had recently been built. Barracks for troops were already in place. They were capable of housing far larger numbers than the small island republic supposedly would ever need. Intelligence sources further implied that a large number of Cuban communists were on hand to train the military.

U.S. Secretary of State George Schultz referred to the "atmosphere of violent uncertainty in the country." He stated further, "We see arrests of leading figures. We see a shoot-on-sight curfew in effect." He denied that the United States was in violation of the Organization of American States charter, which prohibited intervention in the internal or external affairs of other states in the group.

But there was strong criticism for the action. World leaders acted negatively to the attack, as did many Democrats in the U.S. Congress.

The President promised that troops would leave Grenada as soon as an interim government could be set up that would put the country "back on a democratic status, so that elections could give Grenadians a chance to choose for themselves the leaders they want."

He maintained that the military action "was forced on us by events that have no precedent in the Eastern Caribbean and no place in civilized society." It further proved to him that the United States needed a strong military defensive system of its own. Such a system would deter the Soviets or any Third World power from starting an attack. What the space-age technicians came up with surprised everybody.

In March of 1983 the President announced the plan that was officially known as the Strategic Defense Initiative (SDI), quickly dubbed by the press as the Star Wars project. It included laser-beam and satellite weaponry designed to shoot down hostile missiles before they could strike.

President Reagan called the SDI a "vision of the future which offers hope." He further stated that this would "give us the means of rendering nuclear weapons impotent and obsolete." He asked for $26 billion over five years to develop the program.

There were complaints that it would probably take two decades to build the system and that there was no way to estimate accurately the final price tag. Some top U.S. scientists believed SDI would not work. If 95 percent of incoming missiles were intercepted, which would be considered a good defense, the 5 percent that get through would destroy the United States, they said.

Reagan believed there was not much choice as an alternative. Originally the two top powers, the United States and the Soviet Union, relied on balanced defensive and offensive forces. But over the past twenty years the United States had nearly abandoned efforts to develop and deploy defenses against weapons, relying instead almost exclusively on the threat of nuclear retaliation.

Reagan regreted this philosophy. "After World War I, all sorts of rules were made about war and the protection of civilians. And here we are, all these years later, and the principal weapon on both sides is a weapon that is designed mainly to kill millions of civilians—with no discrimination— men, women, and children. How do we think that we're more civilized today when our peacemaking policy is based on the threat that if they kill our people, we'll kill theirs?"

The Star Wars plan would change the perspective, Reagan insisted. "All we're doing is research. And if they really mean it about wanting to eliminate the threat of those weapons and if research can bring us the idea of a weapon that makes these others obsolete, then it's good for them and good for us. . . . I wish that they would go forward with the same thing themselves because if both of us knew we could stop the other fellow's missiles, we wouldn't have to have them anymore."

Reagan was characterized as a gunslinger, a saber rattler. "Nonsense," he replied. "We are showing a determination to maintain a national defense policy. They hadn't seen that before. I think they know now that we are looking at them realistically. . . . In the past we've dealt with them on a mirror-image basis—that well, gee, they're just like us. And if they see that we're nice, why they'll be nice too. I thought it was time that we talked straight."

Some members of Congress felt that such a program would violate the Anti-Ballistic Missile (ABM) treaty with the Soviet Union. It was noted that frequently Reagan's anti-Soviet rhetoric had increased cold-war jitters. And of course, there were some who complained that the enormous sums of money for such a system would be better used for social programs.

Only with the President's strong urging were funds appropriated for the initial development of the system.

President Reagan enjoys a day at his ranch.

Pete Souza, The White House

In spite of such controversial world and national problems, Ronald Reagan was able to maintain his popularity. He projected a boyish enthusiasm and a sincere and earnest patriotism for his country.

Governor Mario Cuomo of New York, a Democrat who frequently disagreed with Ronald Reagan's policies, paid an unusual tribute to the President. "His deportment has been an absolute lesson to the nation in strength, dignity. He never raises his voice, he never gets angry, he's never in a bad humor or very rarely.

"He's struck down by an assailant and makes a joke about it. . . . He has been magnificent. I think it's incalculable the contribution he's made to our moral well-being, just the way he's behaved. He's a lesson to all of us.

"That's part of the role of leader—what Teddy Roosevelt meant when he said the Presidency is a 'bully pulpit.' It isn't just a matter of delivering a speech. It's a matter of communicating a certain style and a certain moral standard. And he's done that magnificently."

In contrast, Nancy Reagan had a much harder time charming the public at first. She was caricatured as a high-handed queen of a newly established aristocracy. Her friends all seemed to be millionaires. Their interests were reported as frivolous and self-serving. At a time when most of the country was suffering through a painful financial recession, Nancy Reagan was pictured wearing excessively expensive gowns and talking about redoing the private rooms of the White House.

Although most of the money was donated by her wealthy friends, the public couldn't imagine spending $800,000 in furnishings and $209,000 on a china service for formal banquets. The fact that the White House was in need of refurbishing was not mentioned in the press.

The criticism hurt her deeply she admits. "I tended to retreat and hold back." She has changed dramatically since those days. From a thin-skinned woman who pouted, even wept when she read criticism about herself in the press, she has emerged as an increasingly confident First Lady with growing clout in the White House. Yet she uses her power not for her own advantage but for her husband. It is for Ronald Reagan's image, his place in history. She is his chief protector.

She was very upset with his staff who had coached him for the first television debate against Jimmy Carter. She offered her own advice. She also suggested that he cancel appearances at army bases to avoid criticism about his strong ties to the military.

Reporters have written that she has an enormous influence on her husband and that she has been the instigator of some of the personnel changes, from the outer office to Cabinet posts. She denies this, although she admits she would have been happier with some changes in the higher ranks. Her husband is a soft touch, she says, who doesn't like to hurt friends even though they're not doing their job well. Obviously she doesn't always get her way, but it is certain that being as close as they are, he listens to her suggestions.

Nancy Reagan gradually learned to turn a deaf ear to petty complaints and to recreate her image as a concerned

The President meets with his Senior Staff. *Left to right:* Donald T. Regan, Edwin Meese, David Stockman, Richard Darman, Robert McFarlane, M.B. Oglesby, Jr., James Baker, Caspar Weinberger, Ronald Reagan.

Bill Fitz-patrick, The White House

and hard-working First Lady. She soon learned that her role might be a grand one but never an easy one. "It's a job," she says, "which I didn't realize."

When she was the governor's wife in California, she had devoted her energies to the Foster Grandparents Program, in which older volunteers befriended orphaned or handicapped children. She had also been interested in the crusade against drug abuse. This was now the project she decided to work with.

At first, critics in Washington claimed that the drug effort was just a public relations gimmick dreamed up by her own staff to make Nancy appear less frivolous. That is definitely not the case. In December of 1980, even before she had moved into the White House, she told Sheila Tate, her former aide, that this was one program she wanted to get involved in. She had lived in California, bringing up two children when the drug problem was just beginning to hit. She became increasingly aware how dangerous it was.

Her antidrug campaign has now taken Nancy Reagan some 70,000 miles to 47 cities in 27 states. Her own self-confidence has increased. She narrated the antidrug documentary "The Chemical People" for PBS, played herself on an episode of *Different Strokes* which dealt with drugs, and was co-host of *Good Morning America* as part of her effort to spur her antinarcotics message. But what she likes best is her contact with young people who have experienced these problems. "The kids relate to me and I to them," she says. She has done a fine job.

"It doesn't mean I've changed as a person. It means I've grown. . . . If you are here and don't grow and don't learn, you are pretty dumb," says Nancy Reagan, "and I don't think I'm dumb."

She's emerged as a person in her own right, not just as the President's wife. She agrees she does feel much more secure now. "It's a combination of things—time, learning more about the job, learning more about the way things work, having gotten over a rough year."

Her husband has been wonderfully supportive. "There's magic to that marriage," David Fisher, the President's personal aide, once told the press. "It's kind of like that magic that's in everybody's courtship has never left the Reagans. . . .They hug and kiss all the time. They're really in love with each other."

Nancy and the President at the Bethesda Naval Hospital.

Terry Arthur,
The White House

Reagan would not consider running for a second term without her approval. She had reservations. "I dragged my heels a little bit," she admits. But when she realized how important it was to him to continue putting his political philosophy into legislation, she agreed and became a successful campaigner herself.

The Democrats chose as their candidate Walter Mondale, who had served as vice president under Jimmy Carter. He was an experienced politician, but he lacked the personal appeal, the speaking ability of Reagan. He ran on a platform that said the only way to control a run-away budget was not so much by cutting spending as by raising taxes. This was obviously not popular news for the voting public.

Many women throughout the country were delighted that Geraldine Ferraro was chosen as his running mate. She did a good job of debating national issues with George Bush, but the press kept emphasizing the fact that she had no experience in world affairs and diplomacy. Would the country be in good hands if by some chance she would have to assume the supreme command of government and military forces if the President were incapacitated?

On November 4, 1984, the people made their choice known at the polls. Ronald Reagan received the greatest vote in the history of the country in the actual number of votes cast for a President as well as receiving an all-time record of electoral votes. Only Walter Mondale's home state of Minnesota and Washington, D.C., gave him their support.

Few would have predicted that such a staunch conservative would win a majority among voters in the ranks of labor, that a candidate who had inspired the term